CAMPAIGN FOR COMEDY!

NOW, ANSWERS TO ALL THE BURNING
POLITICAL QUESTIONS OF THE DAY . . .

WHO?

WHEN?

HOW MANY?

REALLY?

SHE DID?

HE WILL?

WOULD YOU?

From America's #1 bestselling humorist
LARRY WILDE'S
POLITICIANS JOKE BOOK

IT WILL DO YOUR CONSTITUTION
A WORLD OF GOOD!

THE OFFICIAL POLITICIANS JOKE BOOK

LARRY WILDE

Illustrations by Ron Wing

BANTAM BOOKS

TORONTO • NEW YORK • LONDON • SYDNEY • AUCKLAND

I don't know why I pick on all the politicians.
They have provided me with more hours of
merriment . . .

—Will Rogers

THE OFFICIAL POLITICIANS JOKE BOOK
A Bantam Book / September 1984

ISBN 0-553-24369-1

Published simultaneously in the United States and Canada

Bantam Books are published by Bantam Books, Inc. Its trade-
mark, consisting of the words ''Bantam Books'' and the por-
trayal of a rooster, is Registered in U.S. Patent and Trademark
Office and in other countries. Marca Registrada. Bantam
Books, Inc., 666 Fifth Avenue, New York, New York 10103.

PRINTED IN THE UNITED STATES OF AMERICA

O   0 9 8 7 6 5 4 3 2 1

DEDICATION

To Joel Wildman, a resolutely staunch Republican with dynamically Democratic ideals.

CONTENTS

Every time I attend a political dinner,
I make it a rule never to sit next to a
legislator; they never pass anything.
—*Lucille Ball*.

There are two periods when Congress
does not work: One is before the
holidays, and the other is after.

All his life President Reagan said he
wanted to be President in the worst
possible way, and he succeeded
beyond his wildest expectations.

If a woman were elected President of
the United States would her husband
be called the ''first man?''

Every politician knows you should
never get caught in bed with a dead
woman or a live man.

Governmental machinery is the mar-
velous device which enables ten men
to do the work of one.

"What I'm telling you about my
distinguished opponent is more truth
than poultry."

The mistake a lot of Republicans
make is to forget they've been
appointed and think they've been
annointed.

Give a politician a free hand and
he'll put it in your pocket.

If a Democrat found he had cannibals
among his constituents, he would
promise them missionaries for their
Sunday dinner.

Politics is the art of obtaining money
from the rich and votes from the
poor on the pretext of protecting
each from the other.

INTRODUCTION

Will Rogers once said: *The trouble with political jokes is that very often they get elected*.

No profession is more prone to the comedic put-down than politics. People love poking fun at politicians. Perhaps it's because they play with every aspect of our lives and when they raise taxes, cause unemployment, and throw our hard-earned money away on unappreciative foreign countries our only recourse is to ridicule:

> Recently, a large discount store advertised a sale on brassieres. The three basic styles were: Democrat, Republican and Liberal.
>
> A customer approached a sales girl and said, "What strange names for brassieres."
>
> "Not at all," answered the clerk.

1

"The Democrat supports the fallen and uplifts the masses."

"The Republican makes mountains out of molehills."

"And with the Liberals—your cups runneth over."

The privilege of roasting our politicians is simply one more example of our democracy at work. Few nations in the world allow this kind of criticism. When foreigners used to censorship settle in the United States they are aghast to hear Americans joke about the two major political parties. Especially this gag:

What is the difference between a Democrat and a Republican?

A Democrat believes in the exploitation of man by man and a Republican believes in the other way around.

There is a tongue-in-cheek report from the Republican Congressional Committee newsletter describing the basic party differences:

Democrats buy most of the books that have been banned somewhere. Republicans form censorship committees and read them as a group.

Republicans usually wear hats and always clean their paint brushes.

Democrats give their worn out clothes to those less fortunate. Republicans wear theirs.

Republicans employ exterminators. Democrats step on the bugs.

Republican boys date Democratic girls. They plan to marry Republican girls, but feel they're entitled to a little fun first.

Republicans sleep in twin beds— some even in separate rooms. That is why there are more Democrats.

Very often the sense of humor of an entire country can be stimulated or thwarted by its leader. Every schoolboy knows that Abe Lincoln was able to crack jokes even during the darkest days of the Civil War. He once said, ''With the fearful strain that is on me night and day, if I did not laugh, I should die.''

Franklin Roosevelt also recognized the therapeutic value of laughter for he loved telling funny stories. Lyndon Johnson regaled cronies with his ''down to earth'' jokes. But not since Jack Kennedy has there been a President so quick with a quip as Ronald Reagan. Kennedy had a natural wit and was able to evoke spontaneous laughter from audiences. Mr. Reagan, on the other hand, has spent almost fifty years in show business rubbing elbows with the best funny men in Hollywood. An easy delivery and good timing have made him a big laugh getter. Here are some samples:

While visiting Canada hecklers jeered Mr. Reagan during a speech. Prime Minister Pierre Trudeau was quite embarrassed but the President put him at ease by saying, "They must have imported them to make me feel at home."

When the costly B-1 bomber program was received with great opposition, Reagan wisecracked: "How did I know it was an airplane? I thought it was vitamins for the troops."

Right after the assassination attempt Reagan endeared himself to all humor lovers. In the operating room he looked up at the attending surgeons and said, "I hope you're all Republicans!"

And he delivered this beauty at a union dinner: "People often ask what I intend to do for the sick, the senile and the elderly. Well, that's easy. I plan to introduce legislation to see that members of Congress serve only one term."

Everyone is aware of the enormous responsibilities of the world's statesmen. Sometimes the outlook appears so bleak it is a wonder they can survive the pressures. Winston Churchill was once asked to state the qualifications for a politician. Without hesitation he answered:

> It is the ability to foretell what will happen tomorrow, next month, next year—and to explain afterward why it did not happen.

Razzing the public servants relieves the tension. When voters get frustrated and dissatisfied they have to have someone on whom to vent their anger. Who better than politicians and what better way than through humor?

So get ready for a few laughs. Here is a collection of the best political persiflage ever put together for the pure purpose of just plain pleasure.

LARRY WILDE

Court Jester Jibes

No matter what politicians do or say the humor professionals can make light of it. Political satire is an American tradition. Picking on the President, the Congress and the candidates up for elections has always been a prime source of laughter for comedians, cartoonists and wags. The jokes are often biting for they are based on truth and as Shakespeare said, "Jesters do oft prove prophets." Here then are some caustic comments and wily witticisms from America's best known funnymen:

A middle of the road politician is a candidate with a yellow stripe down his back.

—Morey Amsterdam

Nothing beats Reaganomics—though herpes can run it pretty close.

—Art Buchwald

Every time I attend a political dinner, I make it a rule never to sit next to a legislator —they never pass anything.

—Lucille Ball

*　　*　　*

There's only one problem with this year's upcoming Presidential election. One of the nominees has to win.

—Alan King

*　　*　　*

Norm Crosby got screams with these potshots at his *Hope For Hearing* Golf Tournament:

"I came from a tough neighborhood in Boston. There was no in between. Either you became a judge or you went to the chair.

"I was twenty-two years old before I discovered the police were paid by the city.

"I heard a politician on television make a statement, he said, 'Payments are being made to protect criminals. Payments are being made to protect thieves. Payments are being made to protect pushers. And the thing I hate most . . . the payments are always late.'"

*　　*　　*

Ronald Reagan is so old his American Express Card is on stone!

—Phyllis Diller

*　　*　　*

Know what an atheist and Ronald Reagan's economic program have in common? Neither one has a prayer.

—Rich Little

*　　*　　*

Reagan has had so many face lifts when a doctor wants to check his appendix all Reagan has to do is open his collar!

Reagan kept his word on the Cabinet. He said he was going to appoint minorities and he did—a bunch of old millionaires.

—Jan Murray

*　　*　　*

They say Ronald Reagan is an old man. He's not an old man, he's a war hero. He was wounded at Gettysburg.

—Rip Taylor

*　　*　　*

Mark Russell, the brilliant political satirist, describes the Reagan Cabinet: "They're the kind of guys that come home from a white-tie affair and slip into a black-tie."

The day Richard Nixon resigned, I wept. I had to go back to writing my own material.

*　　*　　*

Henny Youngman, known as "King of the One-Liners," often comes up with a longer joke. Here's one of his gems:

Two newlyweds went to Washington D.C. for their honeymoon and decided to check into the Watergate Hotel. The bride got into bed and said, "Honey, I feel so uncomfortable, maybe this room is bugged!"

"But that all happened a long time ago!"

"I can't relax thinking about it."

So the groom began looking behind pictures, into lamps, between furniture. Then he lifted up the rug and found a metal disc on the floor. He removed the screws and pulled up the disc. The relaxed newlyweds now consummated their marriage vows in great style.

Next morning in the lobby the desk clerk asked them, "Did you spend a pleasant night?"

"Oh, yes," replied the groom.

"I'm glad," said the clerk. "The couple in the room right under yours had a chandelier fall down on top of them!"

10

Pat Buttram, the popular TV actor and after-dinner speaker, says, "I always make a silent prayer before I rise. 'Dear Lord, fill my mouth with worthwhile stuff, and nudge me when I've said enough.''

*   *   *

Comedian Nipsey Russell made these political observations on a recent TV show:
"You do not qualify as a citizen of the United States if you're ignorant. If you're illiterate you cannot vote. If you're illiterate or your character is bad you cannot vote in the United States. You can get *elected*. . . . But you cannot vote."

"My dad was a great Democrat. He stole so much money he became a Republican."

*   *   *

Fred Allen was attending a political dinner in New York. The main speaker was a politician who went on and on using tired clichés and fluffy phrases. After more than an hour of saying practically nothing, the politician said: "Well, to make a long story short . . ."
"It's too late now," retorted Allen.

*   *   *

Mort Sahl defines a conservative as one who believes that nothing should be done for the first time.

*　　*　　*

Milton Josefsberg, the veteran TV comedy writer and author of *The Jack Benny Show,* describes this hilarious happening in his best-selling biography of Benny:

"Jack was invited by President Truman to an afternoon affair at the White House in honor of a group of reporters and photographers. Jack knew that he would be called upon to entertain, as he always was, so he brought along his violin as a prop, and he also hoped that he could get Harry Truman to join him in a duet of *The Missouri Waltz.*

As he approached the gate the guard, who not only recognized Jack but had his name listed among those invited, stopped him as a mere formality and asked, "Your name, please?"

"Jack Benny."

The guard pointed to Jack's violin case and asked, "What do you have in there?"

Jack figuring he should live up to his reputation as a comic answered, "I have a machine gun in there."

"Thank heavens!" replied the guard. "I thought it was your violin!"

*　　*　　*

Dick Gregory tells about dreaming that Alabama's George Wallace died and found himself at the entrance to paradise. He knocked on the Pearly Gates for admission.

A deep, black voice from within asked, "Who dat knockin' at de door?"

"Never mind," shouted Wallace, shaking his head. "Never mind."

* * *

Political humor has always played a big part in Republican Bob Hope's comedy routines. Here are some classics:

While visiting Pennsylvania: "I didn't know what the issues were in an election in Wilkes-Barre. I didn't even know there was an election. I was driving through the city and put my hand out to signal a left turn. Immediately, eight candidates shook it."

"The Democrats have an answer to the unemployment problem. They're all running for the presidency."

Bob told this at a Beverly Hills charity dinner:

"I'm happy to see our Governor George Deukmejian get away from his desk for this important evening. George thinks capital punishment is being stuck in Sacramento."

* * *

Then, of course, there was Will Rogers, America's greatest purveyor of political put-downs. He loved to poke fun at the politicians and his audiences responded with raucous laughter and resounding applause. Here are some classics:

I love a dog. He does nothing for political reasons.

Once a man holds public office, he's absolutely no good for honest work.

The further away I get from Washington D.C., the more faith I have in our country.

My little jokes don't hurt nobody. But when Congress makes a joke, it's a law. And when they make a law, it's a joke.

I went to the White House when Warren Harding took over. Wanted to tell him the latest political jokes. He said, "You don't have to, Will. I appointed them."

There is something about a Republican that you can only stand for him just so long. And on the other hand there is something about a Democrat that you can't stand for him quite that long.

*   *   *

Do you get the idea that Richard Nixon is Secretary of State and they don't have the heart to tell us?

—Mark Russell

* * *

Comedians, as well as politicians, often refer to the Father of Our Country. Red Buttons gets screams with this smoothy:

"My ancestor Solomon Schwartz was the only Jew in the boat when Washington crossed the Delaware. All the way across, Uncle Solomon kept moaning to General Washington, 'Everybody spends the winter in Miami Beach. How come we have to spend it in Trenton?' "

Red then usually adds this topper:

"Solomon Schwartz was also the first to predict to Thomas Jefferson and Mrs. Jefferson that someday *The Jeffersons* would be on television."

* * *

Georgie Jessel had been asked to speak on behalf of President Roosevelt in a nationwide broadcast. Jessel was allotted twelve minutes, but preceding speakers had exceeded their time limit and the toastmaster general found himself with ninety seconds remaining at the end of the broadcast.

Here's what he said:

"Ladies and gentlemen, most of my eloquent colleagues have this evening taken up much of their time in expounding the weaknesses and vices of President Roosevelt's opponent, Thomas Dewey. I shall not. I could not do this. I know Governor Thomas E. Dewey, and Mr. Dewey is a fine man."

A low murmur of disapproval spread through the assembled crowd.

Jessel went on: "Yes, Dewey is a fine man. So is my Uncle Morris. My Uncle Morris should not be President, neither should Dewey. Good-night."

*   *   *

A comedian wanted to work with a straight man and was interviewing a young fellow for the job.

"I need a guy who can keep a straight face throughout my performance and who will under no circumstances allow a smile to show on his face no matter what I say or do. Now what are your qualifications for the job?"

"Well," replied the youth, "I used to be a page boy in the House of Representatives."

Lawmaker Levity

"Vote for me!" ranted the Democratic candidate at a political rally. "I'll give you the shirt off my back!"

"Oh, no," hollered a heckler from the back row. "We ain't takin' no more shirt off no more politicians."

* * *

A politician put his young son on top of a ladder and holding out his arms asked him to jump. The little boy leapt and as he did the father stepped aside and the boy crashed to the floor.

"Now, son," said the father. "That'll teach you never to trust a politician."

* * *

Did you hear about the politician who got a crick in his neck trying to save both faces?

* * *

Doctor:	I'm delighted to tell you that you're the father of triplets.
Politician:	Impossible! I demand a recount.

*   *   *

What's a politician's motto in life?
It isn't who you know but who you yes!

*   *   *

A politician in love with a show girl hired a detective agency to check up on her. He received the following report:

The young lady has an excellent reputation. Her past is without a blemish. She has many friends of good social standing. The only scandal associated with her is that she has often been seen lately with a politician of questionable character.

*   *   *

What have politicians and fish in common?
They wouldn't get into trouble if they kept their mouths shut.

*   *   *

The politician was speaking to the local Kiwanis club. He rattled on for over an hour and a half before glancing at his watch and remarking, "They didn't tell me how long I could speak. . . ."

A taxpayer in the back of the room shouted, "There's a calendar right behind you."

*   *   *

The chairman at the annual fund raising dinner for the mayor approached him and said, "Shall we let them enjoy themselves a little longer or do you want to begin your speech?"

*   *   *

POLITICS

As in making love, a lot can be accomplished with a little suction.

*   *   *

The candidate had poured it on for about an hour. Finally, he asked: "Now are there any questions?"

"Yes," came a voice from the rear. "Who else is running?"

*   *   *

John Vandekamp, California's consummate attorney general, was applauded at a Leukemia Society fund raiser for this corker:

A Seattle councilman was giving a fiery speech to a group of longshoremen in order to get reelected. He shouted and bellowed but actually said nothing. Slowly but surely the audience got up and left.

Within twenty minutes the entire crowd was practically gone. As one huge toughie sauntered out of the hall he spotted a man sitting in the last row. "C'mon," he beckoned, "you're not gonna sit there and listen to all that crap, are you?"

"What can I do?" answered the man. "I'm the next speaker!"

A newsman called the governor's office for a copy of a speech to be delivered at a state dinner.

"I am sorry, but I am unable to give you a copy of the governor's speech," said an aide. "I just talked to the man who is writing it and he said the governor is going to talk off the cuff."

*   *   *

Steve Lamb, the nifty Novato homebuilder, tells about the politician who flung down several typewritten sheets before his speechwriter.

"Don't use such big words in my speeches," he said. "I want to know what I'm talking about."

*   *   *

Who is a politician's greatest admirer? His wife's husband.

*   *   *

A state politician showed up in a small eastern Alabama town, and, mounting the courthouse steps, he shouted: "They're wastin' yore tax money a-teachin' Latin and Greek in the schools. That ain't necessary. If English was good enough for Jesus Christ, it ought to be good enough for Alabama."

*   *   *

Upon entering a room in a Washington hotel, a lady recognized a prominent congressman pacing up and down and asked him what he was doing there.

"I'm going to deliver a speech."

"Do you usually get so nervous before making a speech?"

"Nervous," replied the politician, "no, indeed, I never get nervous!"

"Well, then," asked the woman, "what are you doing in the ladies' room?"

*   *   *

POLITICIAN

Someone who is always
me-deep in talk.

*   *   *

Texas has never been known to produce politicians guilty of understatement. One Lone Star State orator climaxes his speech by saying, "No planet in the universe has contributed as many notable figures to history as Texas. Ma Ferguson, Sam Houston, Abraham Lincoln, George Washington, Charlemagne, the twelve Apostles . . ."

"Hole on there, pardner," drawled a big oil man, "only nine of them twelve Apostles was from Texas."

25

Gail Browning, Bantam's beautiful Southwest Regional sales rep, breaks up accounts with this bauble:

During the heat of a spirited election campaign, a friend visiting the Caldwell home declared, "I will never vote for that mudslinging candidate."

The Caldwell's four-year-old daughter, Nora, was present and listened in.

The following afternoon, Mrs. Caldwell caught Nora and a playmate in a mud fight.

"Why, Mommy," said Nora, "we're just playing politics!"

Did you hear about the politician who never told a lie if the truth could do as much damage?

*　　*　　*

A politician once gave two reasons for talking to himself. First, he always liked to talk to a sensible man; second, he liked to hear a sensible man talk.

*　　*　　*

The best after-dinner speech I ever heard was, "Waiter, I'll take the check."
—Adlai Stevenson

*　　*　　*

The newspaper in a small midwestern town printed by mistake that the local politician had died. The next issue contained the following correction:

"We regret that the notice of his death was in error!"

*　　*　　*

Wife: I wish I were ten votes.
Politician: Ten votes? Why?
Wife: Then I would be sure you loved me.

*　　*　　*

A politician at an annual Republican state convention pointed an accusing finger at the chairman and said, "I dare you to reveal the sinister interest that controls you."

"You leave my wife out of this," said the politician.

*   *   *

Five-year-old Jason approached his politician father one evening and asked, "Daddy, what is economics?"

Surprised at his young son's question the politician decided to take extra patience with his answer. "Jason, the best way to explain it is to use symbols. Now Daddy is Capital. Mommy is Government. The maid is Labor. And baby is the Future. Put them all together and you have economics."

Later that night, the youngster awoke and headed for the bathroom. He noticed that his mother was sleeping alone in the bedroom and he spotted his father down the hall in the maid's room. Jason went to the toilet and after a quick peek at his baby brother he went back to sleep.

Next morning at breakfast his father said, "Son, you remember our conversation last night. Now I'd like to ask you if you know what economics is?"

"Oh, sure," said the boy. "While Government is sleeping, Capital is screwing Labor and the Future looks shitty."

*   *   *

A politician was touring Rome with his wife. When he saw the Colosseum he remarked: "Now there's an example of bad planning. I'm certain they never took into account the rising costs of labor and materials. They just didn't have enough dough to finish the job!"

*   *   *

Did you hear about the politician who was so honest and so unimaginative that, since he couldn't tell a lie, he never had anything to say? (He was elected by a landslide vote.)

*   *   *

A traveling preacher was debating with a Texas oilman who doubted the miracle of divine chastisement.

"Let me tell you of a remarkable occurrence," the preacher said. "In this morning's paper, there's an article about a politician who was struck by lightning while he was lying. Miraculous incident, wasn't it?"

"I don't know, now," replied the Texan. "It would be more of a miracle if lightning struck a politician when he wasn't lying."

*   *   *

A recent survey has shown that ninety percent of all politicians were bottle babies.

Which just goes to show that even their own mothers didn't trust them.

* * *

A surgeon, an architect and a politician were arguing as to whose profession was the oldest.

"Gentlemen," said the surgeon, "Eve was made from Adam's rib, and that surely was a surgical operation."

"Maybe," said the architect, "but prior to that order was created out of chaos, and that was an architectural job."

"But," interrupted the politician, "somebody created the chaos first!"

* * *

WARD HEALER'S WALTZ

She was only a politician's daughter, but she said yes to every proposition.

* * *

"Who is your wife going to vote for?"
"For whomever I vote."
"And who are you going to vote for?"
"She hasn't decided yet."

* * *

Lulu Zezas, Wyoming's celebrated cattle queen, loves this kind of cackler:

Baldwin, a candidate for Congress in a ranching community, was out drumming up support among his constituents when he spotted one of them milking a cow. Not one to miss an opportunity, Baldwin grabbed a pail and set out to help.

"That dumb opponent of mine," he began cheerfully, "has he been around to talk to you yet?"

"He sure has," nodded the rancher. "Matter of fact, he's working the other side of this cow right now."

32

"Why did they provide the Capitol with a rotunda?"

"Because politicians love to run around in circles."

*　*　*

The anchorman on a late night TV news program surprised his viewers with this announcement:

"We have good news and bad news for you. First the bad news: Our planet is being invaded by Martians. And now for the good news . . . they eat politicians and pee gasoline."

*　*　*

Filbert, the owner of two lovebirds, sent for a veterinarian. "I'm worried about my birds," he announced. "They haven't gone potty all week."

The doctor looked inside the cage and asked, "Do you always line this thing with maps of the United States?"

"No," answered Filbert. "I put that in last Saturday when I was out of newspapers."

"That explains it!" replied the vet. "Lovebirds are sensitive creatures. They're holding back because they figure this country has taken all the crap it can stand."

*　*　*

A local politician speaking to the group said, "If the leaders of the Democrat and Republican parties were all in a canoe going down the Mississippi River and the boat capsized, who would be saved?"

"The United States!" shouted a man in the crowd.

*   *   *

Did you hear about the ninety-year-old senator who tried to seduce a fifteen-year-old girl?

He was charged with assault with a dead weapon.

*   *   *

Craig and his father were sunning in the backyard when the youngster asked, "Dad, what is a politician?"

"A politician is a human machine with a wagging tongue," replied the father.

"What is a statesman?"

"It is an ex-politician who has mastered the art of holding his tongue."

*   *   *

A college newspaper recently suggested that the marijuana question could easily be settled by a joint session of Congress.

*   *   *

A politician who changed his views rather sharply was congratulated by a colleague. "I'm glad you've seen the light," he said.

"I didn't see the light," came the reply. "I felt the heat."

* * *

A gay politician named Dean
Was caught frolicking in the latrine
    He claimed it was rape
    But they have it on tape
And his smile's positively obscene.

* * *

Try not to confuse Republicans with Democrats. Both of them are already confused.

* * *

A huge, jovial bear of a Democrat running for mayor strode through a hall greeting everybody as a long-lost friend. He slapped one man on the back and said, "Say, I know I've seen your face before."

"Very likely," agreed the voter. "I've been a guard at the county jail for the past thirty years!"

* * *

A politician who was sick in the hospital received a "Get Well" card from the City Council with the following message:

"The decision to send you the card was passed by a vote of six to five!"

* * *

Politician: . . . And so, I say, ladies and gentlemen, we all have cause for concern. Automation is taking away your jobs . . . yes and *my* job too. I can see the day when computers will even replace us politicians!

Heckler: Impossible! Where ya gonna find a machine that breaks promises?

* * *

At a recent political convention the speeches were so boring that all the delegates fell asleep and never got around to nominating a candidate.

* * *

A Sunday school teacher was telling of Jesus's triumphant entry into Jerusalem on a donkey. A youngster in the front row remarked, "I didn't know Jesus was a Democrat."

Wally Haehl, Westamerica Bank's dynamic Gualala director, donated this delightful dandy:

During the gold mining days in California a candidate for Congress hung a sign on a burro reading, "Vote for Duncan for Congress." He lead the donkey through a small mining town and soon a crowd of miners gathered to survey the candidate and the burro.

One of the miners looked at the sign on the donkey, then at the candidate, and said, "Hey, stranger, which one of you is Duncan?"

In Sacramento, an aide of George Deukmejian had to quickly suppress a directive given out by a state official.

Posted on the bulletin board in his office were these inviting words:

EXECUTIVES WHO HAVE NO SECRETARIES OF THEIR OWN MAY TAKE ADVANTAGE OF THE GIRLS IN THE STENOGRAPHIC POOL.

*   *   *

Did you hear about the politician who isn't a Democrat or a Republican?

He's a combination of both. He eats like an elephant and thinks like a jackass.

*   *   *

Grandma came from Georgia fifty years ago and settled in Vermont. Despite a husband, eleven children and twenty-nine grandchildren who voted the straight Republican ticket, Grandma remained a Democrat until her dying day.

She had truly been a political embarrassment to her kin.

And now the undertaker called to confirm the funeral arrangements for the old lady. One son-in-law—who was head of the county Republican party—answered the phone.

"I'm sorry to disturb you," said the

undertaker, "but there appears to be some confusion as to whether the body is to be buried or cremated."

"Let's not take any chances," said the party leader. "Do both."

*   *   *

A Democratic senator seeking votes spoke from the back of the truck. He was in the midst of his spiel when he was heckled, "I'd rather vote for the devil."

"Suppose your friend does not run?" said the senator. "May I count on your support?"

*   *   *

"I've come," said the woman politician, "to ask for you to support me."

"I'm sorry, miss," replied the man, "but you're too late. I've been married for years."

*   *   *

A reporter was about to interview a politician when he noticed three trays on his desk that said: IN, OUT, and L.B.W. "What does L.B.W. mean?" he asked.

"Let the Bastards Wait," replied the politico.

*   *   *

AT AN ALBANY COCKTAIL PARTY

Hostess: You know, I've heard a great deal about you.

Politician: Possibly, but you can't prove a thing.

*   *   *

It's a doggone shame! What kind of justice is there? If dogs make a mess in New York City, they get a fifty dollar fine. If politicians make a mess in New York City, they get a three billion dollar loan.

*   *   *

Before Dr. Manley retired and turned the practice over to his son, he reminded the newly graduated young man, "Sometimes patients in a small town find it hard to describe their symptoms. Others hold back important details out of fear. You gotta keep your eyes open and notice significant details for yourself.

"Take fat Mrs. Pruitt. Only thing wrong with her is that she stuffs herself full of candy. How do I know? You'll always see a dozen half empty boxes scattered all over the house. And Mr. Gunkel. Liquor's the cause of that attack he had last night. I happened to notice an empty gin bottle in his trash basket. By observing details like that, you'll save yourself a heap of diagnosing!"

"I get it," said the son.

As part of the son's medical training the two answered a house call together. They entered the apartment of a beautiful model who was tossing about on her bed.

The new medico listened to her fast heartbeat, felt her fevered hands, but dropped the thermometer when removing it from her mouth. He recovered it quickly and told the young woman, "Nothing wrong with you that can't be cured by cutting down on your political activity. I think you're taking that part of your life too seriously."

When they were back on the street, Doc Manley asked his boy, "Where did you get the notion she was mixing too heavily in politics?"

"I just followed your tip about keeping my eyes open," said the son. "When I reached down to pick up that thermometer I saw the Governor under the bed."

Roasting Ronnie

Two birds were sitting on a telephone pole. "Say," said the first bird, "are you for Reagan?"

"Why not?" answered the other bird. "He's for us!"

*   *   *

Two men were standing together in the waiting room of the Washington D.C. train station making strange hand movements under their coats.

"Look at those two," said a woman to the security guard. "What are they up to?"

"It's all right, they're deaf and dumb. They're just telling each other Ronald Reagan jokes."

*   *   *

Have you heard about Reagan's attempts to cut down the number of government workers? He has a plan that calls for HEW to be run by just two people: Dr. Joyce Brothers and Ann Landers.

*   *   *

Reagan says he's going to stand on his record. But he won't be able to stand on anything until he gets his foot out of his mouth.

*   *   *

A traveling salesman decided to spend the night in a small town out west. After a few drinks at the hotel bar, he loosened up and began spouting his political opinions.

"I tell you," he shouted, "President Reagan is a horse's ass!"

At this, a six foot cowboy stalked over to him and said, "Mister, them's fighting words around here!"

"I'm sorry, sir," stammered the salesman, "I didn't realize that this was Reagan country."

"It ain't," growled the giant, "this here is horse country!"

*   *   *

New York theatrical agent Ken Grayson broke up Catskill comics with this ad-lib:

"Ronnie Reagan has put his foot in his mouth so often he brushes his teeth with a shoehorn."

*   *   *

George Bush was walking past the Lincoln Memorial one day when he heard a ghostly voice saying:

"George bring me a horse. . . . Bring me a horse. . . ."

The same thing happened the next day and the next. The Vice President reported the incident to Reagan and the two men went down to the Lincoln Memorial together to investigate.

Suddenly, the ghostly voice started up again:

"You fool. I said 'Bring me a horse—' and you've brought me an ass."

* * *

The President, Nancy, George Bush and Tip O'Neill were flying across the country on Air Force One. Mr. Reagan turned to Nancy and said, "I think I'll throw this hundred dollar bill out the window and make someone happy."

"That's a good idea," said Mrs. Reagan "but why don't you throw out ten ten-dollar bills and make ten people happy."

George Bush chimed in, "Why don't you throw out a hundred one dollar bills and make a hundred people happy."

At that moment Tip O'Neill snapped, "Why don't you jump out and make everybody happy."

* * *

Rick Minyard, the Los Angeles Lecture Bureau booking impressario, stirs up big boffs with this bubbler:

In order to discover how popular he was Ronnie took Nancy for a drive through the backcountry of West Virginia. They stopped at a farmhouse and knocked on the door.

"What ken Ah do for yer?" asked the farmer.

"Hello," said the President. "Do I look familiar?"

"No," said the farmer.

"I'm from California," said Reagan.

"Ain't that nice."

"I used to make movies."

"My goodness," exclaimed the farmer.

"My initials are R.R."

"Martha!" the farmer shouted to his wife, "You better come on out. Roy Rogers and Dale Evans are here."

CONGRESSIONAL RECORD AD

President Reagan admirer seeks to meet with another President Reagan admirer.
OBJECT: To see if there is another President Reagan admirer.

*   *   *

Did you hear about the Ronald Reagan bra?

Supports the right and ignores the left.

*   *   *

The Donahue's were die-hard Democrats who were having their child christened. At the church, Donahue held the baby. The priest asked for the name of the child. Donahue blurted, ''Reagan!''

Outside, after the ceremony, Mrs. Donahue exclaimed, ''Why did you call him after that man? You know how I dislike the sound of that name.''

''Well,'' replied the Irishman, ''I couldn't resist. As I held the baby in my arms, he started smiling at me. And in a little while he was soaking me.''

*   *   *

Reagan could easily be reelected. When he says something, people know he's not lying—he was never that good an actor.

*   *   *

When Reagan became governor of California, Jack Warner, the movie mogul, declared: "It's our fault. We should have given him better parts."

*   *   *

Holly Mitchell, Hollywood's glamorous stage show producer, hails this humdinger:

A young Kansas City boy wrote this note:

Dear Lord:
I would like to give my mother a birthday present but I have no money so won't you please send me one hundred dollars right away.

The boy addressed the envelope *For God* and slipped it in the mailbox.

Somebody at the Post Office, with a sense of humor, readdressed it to the White House, where it reached the attention of President Reagan. He promptly sent the youngster a check for five dollars with a cheery note clipped to it.

Three days later, the boy wrote another note addressed to God.

Thanks for sending me the hundred dollars I asked for. But why did You send it through Washington? As usual, those darn Republicans deducted ninety-five percent of it!

*   *   *

President Reagan said all his life he wanted to be President in the worst possible way, and he succeeded beyond his wildest expectations.

*   *   *

Janovsky won first prize in the company sales competition—a fishing holiday in the South Sea Islands. When he returned, Janovsky related his travels to the sales vice president.

"What a place," he told him. "The whole island was surrounded by man-eating sharks. Every day I put on my swimming trunks, took my rod and waded into the sea. And there were hundreds of these man-eating sharks all around me."

"Wait a minute," said the vice president. "Don't tell me you went out fishing without a boat when there were man-eating sharks in the water?"

"Sure. They didn't bother me at all," said Janovsky. "I got a tattoo on my chest that says 'Reagan's the Best President Ever' and not even a shark would swallow that."

*   *   *

RONALD REAGAN SANDWICH

You start with bologna and just keep adding more and more.

*   *   *

Reagan and Chernenko were chatting over the hot line one morning when the Soviet leader said:

"Incidentally, Ronnie, I had a dream about Washington last night. I dreamed I saw the White House, and as I watched, the Stars and Stripes was lowered and in its place flew a big red flag."

"Oh, really?" replied Reagan, "Well, I had a dream last night, too, Konstantin. I was standing in Red Square looking at the Kremlin, and there over the top flew a big red banner with writing on it."

"That's not unusual," said Chernenko, "What did the writing say?"

"I don't know, Konstantin. I can't read Chinese."

*   *   *

Did you hear about the new Ronald Reagan bucket at the Kentucky Fried Chicken? It's full of right wings and assholes.

53

White House Waggery

The Kimberlys, visiting from Kansas, were walking past the White House one evening.

"For just two people," said the husband, "they sure burn enough lights."

*   *   *

Two men were chatting at a Washington cocktail party. "Have you heard the latest White House joke?" asked one man.

"No," said the second, "and before you begin, I think you oughta know that I work at the White House."

"That's okay," said the first man. "I'll tell it very slowly."

*   *   *

Three reporters were arguing over the true meaning of prestige in Washington.

"Prestige is when you're at a party and you get a phone call from the President because he needs your advice," said one newsman.

"No," said the second. "Prestige is when you're invited to go down to the Oval Office and talk to the President personally."

"You've got it all wrong," said the third. "Prestige is when you are in the Oval Office, talking to the President, and the phone rings. He picks it up, listens for a minute, and then says, 'It's for you!' "

* * *

PRESIDENTIAL PRAYER

The more I examine the world's sorry mess,
The more I would like to be President less!

* * *

The television anchorman approached the White House press secretary and asked how things were progressing.

"Just think of the President and Congress as the married couple next door," he replied. "This will give you a much better understanding of what's going on."

* * *

The wife of one of our Vice Presidents accompanied him on one of his South of the Border goodwill trips. Back at the White House her daughter asked her, "What did you eat down there?"

She answered, "Lots of beef, spicy side dishes and 7,886 green peas."

"Quit kidding me, Mom," protested the daughter. "How would you know exactly how many peas you ate?"

"Young lady," answered the Vice President's wife, "how do you suppose I occupy my time while your father's speaking?"

*   *   *

A man went to a Washington psychiatrist and complained, "Doctor, I'm in rough shape. I'm in politics, but I can't make a decision, I can't give a speech, I'm losing my friends, I'm not sure of what I'm doing. Everything seems to be going wrong."

"Then why don't you get out of politics?" asked the psychiatrist.

"I can't," said the politician. "You see, I'm the President."

*   *   *

Why did Jimmy Carter carry a turkey around with him?

For spare parts.

*   *   *

Sondra Wildman, New Jersey's foremost nutritionist, loves this nifty nugget:

One spring afternoon a tourist noticed a man alone out in a rowboat on the Potomac, shouting, "No! No! No!"

"Nothing to worry about," said a passing policeman. "He's just a White House 'Yes man' on vacation."

You can tell Jimmy Carter is proud he's from the South. He had the Oval Office repaneled in okra.

*   *   *

Some psychiatrists claim that if you listen closely to what a youngster says very often you can tell that he's Presidential timber:

When Jimmy Carter was a little boy his father asked him, ''Were you the one who chopped down the peanut plant?''

''Father, I cannot tell a lie,'' replied Jimmy, ''maybe I did and maybe I didn't!''

*   *   *

Mr. Carter once called in one of his bright young Georgia assistants and said, ''The people want to know what we are going to do about the farm bill.''

''I don't have that file with me,'' replied the Georgian, ''but you can tell the people, if we owe it, we will pay it.''

*   *   *

Did you hear about the ex-President doll?

You wind it up and it writes memoirs.

*   *   *

Jerry Ford moved to Palm Springs, California, because he wants to be near this country's real seat of power—Frank Sinatra's house.

*   *   *

Nixon was out walking along a New Jersey beach and decided to go for a swim. He got out beyond the waves and suddenly began drowning.

Three teenage boys happened along, dove into the ocean and pulled Nixon ashore. When he had regained his breath, Nixon thanked the boys. In appreciation, he said, "I'd be willing to use my influence to help you boys in any way I can. Is there anything special you want?"

"I'd like to go to West Point!" said one boy.

"I believe I can arrange that!" said the ex-President.

"I'd like to go to Annapolis!" said another boy.

"I'll see to it immediately," said Nixon.

"I'd like to be buried in Arlington Cemetery," announced the third boy.

"That's a very strange request," said Mr. Nixon. "Why would you ask now to be buried in Arlington Cemetery?"

"Well," said the youngster, "when I get home and tell my father who I saved from drowning, he's gonna kill me!"

*   *   *

Comedian Shamus M'Cool gets great results with these two goodies:

"Did you see that Jimmy Carter wrote his memoirs? We're trying to forget him and he's making us remember!

Time paid him a great tribute. They put his book on the fiction and nonfiction list."

*　　*　　*

"I just saw former President Nixon in church praying.

"Oh, really? To whom?"

*　　*　　*

Richard Nixon's tapes have revealed a conversation that was supposed to have taken place with Bob Haldeman.

"Bob, I realize that some day I'm going to pass on," said the former president to his aide. "I'd like you to find a nice burial place for me."

Two weeks later, Haldeman returned and said, "Mr. President, I've found just the spot. It's on a hill overlooking a beautiful stream. And the sun hits it during the day almost as if you were being spotlighted."

"Sounds good," said Nixon. "How much?"

"$400,000!"

"What? $400,000!" cried Nixon. "I'm only gonna be there three days!"

*　　*　　*

Ronald Reagan once said of Mr. Ford, "Jerry is a completely modest man—and with very good reason."

* * *

During a recent vacation in the Rockies, Gerald Ford picked up a rattlesnake and killed a stick.

* * *

Nixon, Ford and Carter were riding on a train when it stopped in a long, dark tunnel. In order to get the train moving again Nixon went up to the engine and bribed the engineer to move.

Then Ford pardoned him.

When the train still didn't move, Carter pulled down the blinds, sat down and said, "I think we're moving now."

* * *

During the early days of Lyndon Johnson's reign, a group of disgruntled aides was leaving the leader's office. "You know," said one, "sometimes I wish he was the Pope instead of the President."

"Why?" asked another in the group.

"Because," came the fast reply, "then we'd only have to kiss his ring."

* * *

Tommy Moore, Pennsylvania's premier comedy performer, kindles howls with this hunk of hilarity:

Valerie, a twenty-three-year-old steno, walked along the beach despondent. She was flat chested and felt totally distraught watching the other big-bosomed girls on the beach surrounded by eligible men. As Valerie strolled on the sand her toe kicked a small bottle. She picked it up and removed the cork. Out popped a genie.

"Who are you?" asked the frightened girl.

"I am a genie. And because you were kind enough to give me my freedom I will grant you any wish you make."

"Oh, that's wonderful," declared Valerie. "I'd like the two biggest boobs in the world."

The genie snapped his fingers and there appeared Jimmy Carter and Jerry Ford.

Jerry Ford is a nice man, but he's hard to please. He never says anything when he talks—and then complains because nobody quotes him.

* * *

Although Eleanor Roosevelt had many qualities that were truly beautiful she was not physically attractive. F.D.R. loved hearing stories about her lack of beauty:

Mrs. Roosevelt boarded a train in Washington late one night and was escorted to an upper berth.

Eleanor climbed up, stretched out and tried to sleep. However, a man in the lower berth was snoring intolerably. His loud snorts became so unbearable the President's wife leaned over and jabbed the man with her umbrella. He awoke immediately, looked up at her and said, "It won't do you no good lady, I had a good look at you when you got on the train."

* * *

Eleanor returned to the White House from a medical checkup, and reported to FDR that her health was fine.

"But," asked Roosevelt, "didn't the doctor say anything about that big fat ass of yours?"

"No, Franklin," replied Eleanor, "he never mentioned your name once."

* * *

Jerry Ford broke up a fund-raising dinner with this observation: "Ronald Reagan doesn't dye his hair; he's just prematurely orange."

*   *   *

Plastic surgeons Schwan, Osterman and Kern met at a medical convention and each man began bragging about his enormous success in reconstructing the human body.

"I operated on a girl a few years ago who was in a terrible automobile accident and I restored her body so perfectly she was in the Miss America contest," said Schwan.

"Well, gentlemen," said Dr. Osterman. "They brought me a boy several years ago who fell off a bridge. He had every bone in his body broken and I put him back together so well he is entered in the Olympics as a Decathlon runner."

"You guys sure have done great work," said surgeon Kern, "but neither of you has accomplished what I have. All I had to work with was a horse's ass and some orange hair and gentlemen, today that man is in the White House."

*   *   *

Nancy Reagan just ordered fifty boxes of Kennedy panty hose—they're guaranteed not to run.

*   *   *

Mr. Reagan does have a sense of humor. In spite of the public opinion polls he recently said, "My esteem in the country has gone up substantially. It is very nice now that when people wave at me, they use all five fingers."

Dirty Politics

A Democratic senator who recently had to visit Kansas City for a committee hearing wanted to take a female acquaintance along.

"I have senatorial immunity," he explained, "so you needn't be afraid of the Mann Act."

"Afraid of it?" she cooed. "Why, Senator, I just adore it."

Miss Kowalski bought a new washing machine but in a few weeks it went on the blink. She phoned the dealer and said, "Sometimes it runs too fast, sometimes too slow."

"Well," he asked her, "did you screw the governor?"

"Why no," said Miss Kowalski, "I didn't even vote for him."

* * *

During one of the school integration crises down south this exchange took place in the corridors of the United States Senate building.

A northern white senator was passing a Dixiecrat senator in the corridor and noticed him wink at a beautiful black girl.

"Why," said the northerner, "I thought you didn't believe in integration."

"I don't," replied the southerner. "You northerners never understand anything. I don't want to go to school with that girl—just to bed with her!"

* * *

A recent survey showed that Democrats generally have more children than Republicans, which is not too hard to believe. After all, who ever heard of anyone enjoying a good piece of elephant?

70

*   *   *

A Milwaukee woman telephoned the police station and exclaimed, "There's a Democrat standing in the window of an apartment across the way masturbating!"

"Lady," said the desk sergeant, "how do you know he's a Democrat?"

"Because," replied the woman, "if he was a Republican he'd be out somewhere screwing somebody!"

*   *   *

A woman's three daughters got married the same day, and all spent the first night of their honeymoon at her home. Next morning she asked them what they thought of married life.

"Well," said the first, "with my husband it was just like with Churchill: 'Blood, sweat and tears.' "

"Mine was like Roosevelt," said the second daughter. "Again and again and again."

"Mine was like Jimmy Carter," said the third girl. "When he thought he was in he was out, and when he finally did get in, he didn't know what to do there."

*   *   *

Doug Galloway, the jovial Alhambra Jolson buff, cheers this jigger of jocularity:

Bandini was psychotically jealous of his sexy wife. One afternoon he came home unexpectedly and found her in the sack, completely nude. Bandini searched under the bed and in all the closets for his wife's lover but without success. Then he dashed madly into the bathroom and threw back the shower curtain. There stood his neighbor Giordano, stark naked.

"What the hell're you doin' here?" demanded the Italian.

"Would you mind closing the curtain?" asked Giordano. "I ain't finished voting yet."

Regina and Sally, two pretty stenos, were discussing their host at a cocktail party.

"The congressman's a remarkable thinker," gushed Regina. "Tell me, don't you find him penetrating?"

"Not if I keep my legs crossed," sneered Sally.

* * *

"Congressman," asked one of his aides during a luncheon meeting, "what do you intend doing about the abortion bill?"

"Shh, not so loud," gulped the legislator. "Phone that quack and tell him I'll pay it first thing next month."

* * *

Upon learning that the attractive call girl he had engaged for the night was an ex-English teacher, the elderly Republican legislator quipped, "Teacher, may I?"

"In your case," she retorted, "it should be 'Can I?'"

* * *

Did you hear about the establishment near Congress in our nation's capitol that caters to kinky tastes?

Naturally, there's a House whip in attendance.

* * *

A reporter was interviewing an outspoken, strong women's libber on her political views. "We believe in capital punishment," asserted the feminist, "but we don't believe women should be hung like men."

*   *   *

Last election day, Phil and George were sitting at their office desks. Suddenly Phil picked up the phone and dialed a number. "Charlie, have you voted yet?" asked Phil. "You'd better hurry if you want to beat the last-minute crowd."

After Phil hung up, George said, "I didn't know you were interested in politics."

"I'm not," said Phil. "That guy is married to the best piece of ass in town, and I'm sneaking over to his house while he's gone."

*   *   *

The candidate for mayor stood before his attentive audience at the political rally, "Although there are two dozen houses of ill fame in our town," he said, "I have never gone to one of them."

"Which one?" called out a heckler from the back of the auditorium.

*   *   *

Did you heard about the senator who was so old that when he chased his secretary around the desk, he couldn't remember why?

*   *   *

High school seniors from several counties were invited to the state capitol to participate in mock-government week. The only thing was the teenagers got more involved in sex than in serious politics.

When one boy returned home, his mother asked, "What was your particular project?"

"It was a battle for the legislative committee posts, Mom," he replied. "There was a nice little split in the opposition—and, I, er, managed to get my member in."

*   *   *

OLD POLITICAL AXIOM

Never get caught in bed with
a dead woman or a live man.

*   *   *

Did you hear about the FBI agent who was given the job of shadowing a gay liberation leader but was fired because he blew his assignment?

*   *   *

Charlotte had been married only three days but now she sat in the office of a marriage counselor.

"What seems to be the trouble?" he asked.

"Oh, Doctor, I'm married to a Democrat," cried the young woman.

"Come now," said the shrink. "What's so bad . . .?"

"It's very frustrating," she explained. "He just sits on the bed, and all I get are promises, promises, promises . . ."

* * *

While the bill was debated, Miss Snyder
Had a Senator thrusting inside her
    To a knock on the door,
    She replied from the floor,
"Go away—I'm attached to a rider!"

* * *

Garibaldi and Ryan, two old friends, met just after the Presidential election.

"Say," said Garibaldi, "I hear they're selling toilet paper with the President's initials on them."

"Why's that?" asked Ryan.

"So the assholes can see who they voted for!"

* * *

77

There was a reason why the elderly Congressman named his new baby Justin. On their wedding night he asked his bride, "Is it in?"

"Just in," she replied.

*   *   *

A man named Harry Peters was running for attorney general of the state. On election day, Peters's campaign manager was standing outside the polling place, asking people for their support. He stopped one woman and inquired, "Do you like Harry Peters?"

"I love them," she answered. "Meet me around in the alley right after I vote."

*   *   *

An overweight senator in Japan on a trade delegation passed a shop that advertised:

LOSE 10 POUNDS IN 15 MINUTES.
ONE YEN.

Intrigued, he entered, paid his yen and was ushered into the presence of a beautiful young girl, completely naked except for a sign hanging from her waist: "If you can catch me, you get this."

After fifteen fruitless minutes of pursuing the adroit and speedy damsel, the puffing, sweating senator left the place, sexually frustrated but, indeed, ten pounds lighter.

The next day he passed another shop, in the window of which was a card reading:

LOSE 20 POUNDS IN 15 MINUTES.
TWO YEN.

He entered, paid his two yen and was immediately confronted by an enormous, ugly sumo wrestler who advanced upon him menacingly.

The brutish wrestler was naked except for a sign dangling in front of his loins. It read, "If I catch you, you get *this*."

*   *   *

If women take over politics, it will cut the cost of eating out. Instead of hundred-dollar-a-plate dinners, they'll serve box lunches.

*   *   *

A young Washington beauty sat in the doctor's office after an examination.

"Miss," announced the M.D., "you're pregnant!"

"What!" exclaimed the girl. "That bastard swore he had diplomatic immunity!"

*   *   *

Stopping to pay a call on some of his surburban constituents, the Democratic congressman discovered they were having a party and offered to come back at a more convenient time.

"Don't go," implored the host. "We're playing a game you might like. We blindfold the women, and then they try to guess the identity of the men by feeling their genitals."

"How dare you suggest such a thing to a man of my dignity and stature!" roared the Democrat.

"You might as well play," said the host. "Your name's been guessed three times already."

80

A congressman and his wife were lying in bed. "All you ever want to do is talk about politics," complained the wife. "For heaven's sake, can't you talk about anything else?"

"Like what, for example?" asked her husband.

"Why don't you talk about sex for a change?"

"All right," he replied. "How often do you think the President has intercourse?"

*   *   *

A Westport, Connecticut Republican committeewoman returned from New York City to party headquarters disheveled and distraught.

"What happened to you?" asked a fellow Republican woman.

*   *   *

"I was in Times Square at the same time the Democrats were holding a rally. The mobs were thick and disorderly. Suddenly, two thugs grabbed me and pulled me into an alley. They tore off my clothes and raped me. It was horrible."

"Didn't you scream?" asked the Republican co-worker.

"What, and have the Democrats think I was cheering for them?"

*   *   *

At a political rally, a spokeswoman for equal rights for women brought down the house with this final rallying cry: "While we women are split the way we are, the men will always be on top."

*   *   *

A newcomer to Washington was confused and disheartened by all the red tape. One night in his hotel room he phoned down to the desk clerk. "Send me up a blonde, a bedpan and a violin—I don't know whether I want to diddle, piddle or fiddle."

*   *   *

Paul, a state senator, and Alice, his gorgeous secretary, broke their engagement. Their friends were shocked. "What happened?" asked a cohort.

"Would you marry someone who was habitually unfaithful, who lied at every turn, who was selfish and lazy and sarcastic?"

"Of course not," said the friend.

"Well," said Paul, "neither would Alice."

*   *   *

Did you hear about the handsome bachelor Senator who hired a ravishing blonde as his assistant and then made her the object of a long congressional probe?

A cameraman from Hohokus
Tried to capture the mayor in focus.
   It turned out a loss,
   For he pictured the boss
With six aldermen kissing his *tokus*.

*　　*　　*

A member of the California legislature had been investigating pornography in that state.

Invited to speak to a San Diego women's club he proceeded to castigate X-rated movies. "My committee saw a movie last night that included rape, homosexuality, lesbianism—in fact, almost every kind of perversion you could think of. It was a disgrace to the human eye."

Then he concluded, "And now, ladies, are there any questions?"

In unison, three women shouted, "Where's it playing?"

*　　*　　*

The attractive blonde hooker had spent the entire evening with the congressman and so he was surprised by the small fee she requested.

"It's not my place to advise you in such matters, miss, but you're not doing yourself justice," said the legislator. "Besides, I frankly don't know how you manage to get by on payments as small as this."

"Oh, it balances out," said the pretty pro. "You see, I do a little blackmailing on the side."

*　　*　　*

Nonooki, the Eskimo prostitute, is thinking of going into politics. She's had a lot of experience giving snow jobs.

*   *   *

The governor arranged the marriage of his daughter to the son of the mayor of the state's largest city—a bond that would unite two important factions of the party. Yet, because the young couple seemed so formal to each other the state leader was worried that the union wouldn't be a success. He posted a spy outside the mansion's bridal chamber, and demanded a full report of the wedding night.

"It is hard to tell," said the governor's spy the next morning. "When the boy came out of the bathroom, I heard the girl say, quite formally, 'I offer you my honor!' Then the boy said, with equal courtliness, 'Madame, I honor your offer.' And that's the way it went all night long—honor, offer, honor, offer.''

*   *   *

Did you hear about the Nevada madam who decided to run for Congress?

Her supporters held a fund raising dinner. It cost a hundred dollars an hour.

*   *   *

The politician was telling some of his constituents, "We are sending three million dollars worth of contraceptives to India."

"Say," one fellow hollered, "couldn't they just do what my wife does—pretend she's asleep?"

*   *   *

Many years ago, a man named Mitchell ran for governor on a ticket to get liquor back in his state. Unfortunately the posters they spread around the country ruined him. They read:

VOTE FOR MITCHELL
AND HAVE ALL YOUR WET DREAMS
COME TRUE.

*   *   *

At a capitol cocktail party a Supreme Court judge and a diplomat from a European country were chatting in a corner.

"How do you expect to settle all this discord between the Democrats and the Republicans?" asked the diplomat.

"I believe love is the ultimate peacemaker," replied the judge. "It eventually softens all hard feelings."

*   *   *

Did you hear about the young girl who married the elderly senator?

She found out it was the same old thing, weak in and weak out.

*   *   *

What has eighteen legs and a vagina?
The Supreme Court.

*   *   *

Dalton, a young Democrat eager to gather votes, accepted the invitation of a local women's club to speak on the subject of sex. Fearing his wife wouldn't understand, Dalton told her he planned to lecture on sailing.

The morning after the speech, Mrs. Dalton met one of the ladies of the club, who mentioned how entertaining his talk had been.

"I can't understand it," said Mrs. Dalton. "He knew so little about it."

"Oh, come now dear. His talk showed a superior knowledge of the subject," said the matron.

"But he's only tried it twice," protested Mrs. Dalton. "The first time he lost his hat, and the second time he got seasick."

*   *   *

Len Krasner, the noted New York State University psychology professor, is partial to this nutty nib of nonsense:

A college celebrating the fiftieth anniversary of its first commencement invited a governor, its most prominent alumnus, to make a speech.

"It was fifty years ago that our class had its commencement," he began. "Those fifty years have truly flown by. But on this occasion, with old friends around me, the hands of the clock are turned back, and I see myself on a moonlit night, sitting out there near the football stadium."

"There was an apple tree nearby and on that night fifty years ago, I sat beside a pretty girl with the moon full above and the apple blossoms overhead. We were both caught up with the romance of the evening and I made love to that girl. If that young lady, now grown a little older in years, should happen to be in this audience and is no more ashamed of that memorable night than I am, I wish she would rise."

Twenty-six gray-haired ladies stood up.

DEMOCRATIC DITTY

She was only a politician's daughter,
but, Boy, could she kiss your baby!

* * *

An elderly prostitute stood before the newly elected magistrate. After listening to her appeal for lenience the judge felt bad about sentencing her. He ordered a short recess, then went to the chambers of an older judge. "Say, Caldwell," he asked, "what would you give a sixty-year-old prostitute?"

"Oh," said the learned jurist, "not anything more than five bucks."

* * *

"I heard the President's wife is gonna get a divorce."

"Really? Why?"

"She claims he's not doing to her what he's doing to the whole country!"

* * *

The secretaries in Washington are now wearing buttons that read:

I CAN TYPE

* * *

"If I became head of the Democratic party I'd change the emblem from a donkey to a condom!"

"Why's that?"

"Because it stands for inflation, limits production, encourages cooperation, and gives you a feeling of security, although you know you're being screwed."

*　　*　　*

The Democratic senator had three unmarried daughters and countless nieces. Yet none of the women was on the public payroll. A reporter asked him to explain this phenomenon.

"An elected official has the duty to maintain high standards of conduct," replied the lawmaker. "No breath of scandal should touch his working staff."

"Then," asked the newsman, "you don't believe in handing out jobs to relatives?"

"No," replied the senator, "I hire only virgins."

*　　*　　*

THE GOOD OLD DAYS

When a politician didn't kiss a lady's baby until after it was made.

*　　*　　*

A woman stopped at the White House gate and said to the guard on duty, "I insist on intercourse with the President."

"Hey, lady," said the guard. "Don't you mean an interview?"

"No, I mean intercourse," she continued. "I want to see the nuts that are screwing the country."

*   *   *

The elderly senator told his hot-bodied young bride, "Baseball season starts tomorrow, and I've been invited to throw out the first ball."

"For all the good you've done me lately," she retorted, "you might as well throw them *both* out."

*   *   *

A young Republican mayor took $200,000 from the city's safe and lost it on a real estate deal. Then his beautiful wife left him. In despair, he went down to the river and was about to jump off the bridge when he was stopped by a wrinkled-faced, stringy gray haired woman in a black cloak.

"Don't jump," she rasped. "I'm a witch, and I'll grant you three wishes if you do something for me!"

"I'm beyond help," he replied and told her his troubles.

"Don't be silly," she said. "Abracadabra! The money is back in the city hall vault. Abracadabra! Your wife is home waiting for you with love in her heart. Abracadabra! You now have $400,000 in the bank."

"That's w-w-wonderful!" stuttered the mayor. "What do I have to do for you?"

"You must spend the night making love to me."

The thought of sleeping with the toothless old hag was repellent, but it was certainly worth it, so they retired to a nearby motel.

In the morning, the distasteful ordeal over, the mayor was getting dressed when the bat in the bed say, "Say, sonny, how old are you?"

"I'm forty-four," he replied. "Why?"

"Ain't you a little old to believe in witches?"

Government Goofs

"How many are working in the civil service?"

"About one in three."

*　　*　　*

"Cooper has gone to his everlasting rest."

"What did he do? Die or take a job with the government?"

*　　*　　*

A civil servant invited out to lunch was asked if he would like coffee.

"I never take coffee after lunch," said he. "It keeps me awake all afternoon."

*　　*　　*

Walter: And your brother, the one who was trying so hard to get the government job, what's he doing now?

Richie: Nothing. He got the job.

*　　*　　*

Dorothea Gray, California's consummate theatrical booker, tells about the group of tourists who were looking down into the depths of the Grand Canyon.

"Did you know," said the guide, "that it took over five million years for this great canyon to be carved out of the rocks?"

"Oh?" said one of the sightseers, "I didn't know this was a government project."

*　　*　　*

Why is a county supervisor the greatest proof of the doctrine of reincarnation?

Because nobody could get that stupid in one lifetime!

*　　*　　*

Geller boarded a suburban train in which two men were already sitting. One of them had a peculiar mannerism, he scratched his elbow again and again.

"Your friend is really badly off," Geller said to the other man when the victim got off at his station.

"Yeah, he's got a terrible dose of piles."

"I didn't know about the piles. I meant all that scratching."

"Yeah, that's the piles! See, he's a civil service worker and he can't tell his ass from his elbow."

At least someone in the Statistics Office of the Labor Department has a sense of humor.

A TV newscaster called to learn the latest unemployment figures.

His question was answered quickly by a clerk, who added, "That's everyone who isn't working, but there are even more if you count the people employed by the Post Office."

* * *

Matson was sent by the Farm Bureau to inspect some midwestern farms. He knew nothing whatever about animals, so when he came across his first goat he just plain didn't know what it was. He wired his chief in Washington: "Have found an animal with a sad face, a long beak, chin whiskers, a skinny frame and a bare rump. What is it?"

The reply came at once. "Animal you describe is a farmer. Be nice to it. It votes."

* * *

ELEPHANT

A mouse built to government specifications.

* * *

Norvel Carrick, the super ARA Services Book Manager, splits sides with this spirit lifter:

On a government road job Panelli, a political job holder, was told to go up the road and warn motorists that the way was partially blocked and to drive carefully.

Panelli was assigned that duty even though he had laryngitis. A car pulled up and Panelli stopped it.

"What's the matter?" asked the motorist.

"There's a government road job up ahead," whispered Panelli because of his hoarse throat.

"That's all right," whispered the driver. "I'll go by quietly so I won't wake them!"

Republican Councilman:	My son says he would like a job in your department.
Commissioner:	What can he do?
Republican Councilman:	Nothing.
Commissioner:	That simplifies it. Then we won't have to break him in.

*　　*　　*

Murphy and O'Flynn had gotten their jobs through Democratic political pull. They were just standing around when the foreman approached them.

"And what are you two fellas doin'?" he asked.

"We're carrying these boards over to that lumber pile," replied Murphy.

"But where are the boards?" asked the foreman.

"How do you like that, O'Flynn? We forgot the boards!"

*　　*　　*

An official very high in the Pentagon proudly displays this sign on his desk:

IF YOU'RE LOOKING FOR A LITTLE INFORMATION, JUST ASK ME. I HAVE AS LITTLE AS ANYONE ELSE IN THIS PLACE!"

Six federal project workers were carrying the accident victim into an undertaker's establishment. The undertaker was quite angry.

"Why," he shouted, "didn't you bring this man's body here at three o'clock, as you promised? It's now after six."

"Sorry," replied the leader, "but we had to wait until the five o'clock whistle blew to find out which of the men was dead."

* * *

Martinez and Castillo, two city workers, were off in a binge. "I'm gonna leave this job and I want you to come with me," said Martinez after his twelfth beer.

"Oh, yeah?" said Castillo.

"Yeah. I know a place in Africa where there's a lot of gold just lying around waiting for someone to pick it up."

"I knew there was a catch to it."

"What's the catch?"

"You gotta bend over!"

* * *

On an Illinois political road-mending scheme the foreman ran short of shovels, so he wired Springfield for them. A smart civil servant sent back the following telegram: Regret have no shovels available. Tell men to lean on each other.

Bill Waysack, Imperial Golf Club big-wig, gets big boffs with this bit of burlesque:

Fulmer was digging on a public works project. "Hey, Puluski," he said to his foreman, "I dug this hole where I was told to and put the dirt back like I was supposed to. But all the dirt won't go back in. What am I gonna do?"

"There's only one thing to do," said the Polack. "You'll have to dig the hole deeper."

The government works foreman started bawling out Fanelli.

"We've had slow men on this job," he said, "but you are the slowest person I've seen. Aren't you quick at anything?"

"Yeah," yawned the workman. "Nobody can get tired as quick as I can."

* * *

Way back in the days of the WPA a Democratic worker had been shifted from one job to another only to have the men complain to the foreman that they couldn't work near him because of his halitosis.

Finally the foreman said, "Listen, Luigi, I don't wanna hurt your feelings but the boys refuse to work with you because of your bad breath."

"Hey," said the Italian, "if-a you had-a to kiss as many Republican asses as I did to get-a this job, your breath would-a smell bad too!"

* * *

Civil Servant: (engrossed in newspapers) More coffee please.

Wife: Isn't it time you went to the office?

Civil Servant: I thought I was in the office.

* * *

A Senate investigation committee was questioning a civil service worker in Washington. "What do you do here?" asked the chairman.

The clerk, fed up with red tape, buck-passing, forms, office politics, and efficiency experts, exclaimed, "I don't do a darn thing."

The committee members made notes, and then interviewed the second clerk. "And what's your job here?" asked the committee leader.

"I don't do a thing, either."

"Ah-hah!" said the Senator in charge, "Duplication!"

*   *   *

A dinner was being held for the new governor. The grizzled old county chairman, who had never seen the new boss, turned to the lady next to him. "Don't tell me that mug is the governor!"

"I think you're impudent and crude," she said icily. "Do you know who I am?"

The county leader shook his head.

"I am the governor's wife."

"Do you know who I am?" he countered.

"No," she said stiffly.

"Good," he replied. "My job is still safe."

Richard Levine, the jocular Justice Department legal whiz, wows friends with this wacky whimsy:

"Our files are so crowded," said the chief clerk to a bureau head in congressional communications, "that we'll simply have to destroy all correspondence more than six years old."

"Go ahead and do it," said his bureaucrat boss. "But first be sure to make copies of everything marked for destruction."

* * *

The postmaster general called a meeting of his top-level postal executives to determine if some way could be found to lessen the problems of mail delivery.

"I've been listening patiently for three hours," he said in exasperation, "and all I want is a simple answer to a simple question: If it is neither snow nor rain nor heat nor gloom of night that stays the couriers from the swift completion of their appointed rounds, then just what the hell is the trouble?"

* * *

POSITION WANTED

Presently employed at City Hall;
will work if I have to.

* * *

BUREAUCRAT

A person who proceeds in a straight
line from an unknown assumption to a
foregone conclusion

* * *

Forsythe, a senior civil servant at the Department of Agriculture, was sent to work on a farm to get some firsthand experience. Beldon, the owner, decided to give him a tough time, so he showed him a large pile of manure and a four-acre field, gave him a fork and a shovel and told him to get on with it. The farmer was surprised to see that the whole lot was spread by the end of the first day.

Next day, Beldon decided to give the civil servant a simpler task. He told him to sort a huge pile of potatoes into small, medium and large.

At the end of the morning the farmer returned and found Forsythe sitting with his hands on his head with very few potatoes sorted.

"Whatcha doin'?" asked the farmer.

"Look," he replied, "I'll spread bull-shit, but these damned decisions are driving me nuts!"

Malaprop Merriment

Fluffs and verbal errors usually result in gales of laughter especially when spoken by a public official. Audiences seem to delight in slips of the tongue by the celebrated. Here are some of the most ludicrous malaprops committed by some of our best known politicians:

At an election campaign dinner, the mayor of a midwestern town caused a mild uproar when he berated his opponent like this: "I happen to know that this guy's wife is a lymphomaniac!"

*   *   *

"Governor," asked a TV reporter, "what is your opinion on the abortion issue?"
"My attitude has always been *déja vu*— whatever will be, will be."

*   *   *

Politician at election meeting: "And I can promise you all this without the slightest fear of verification."

*   *   *

A candidate for the Illinois Senate was addressing a Republican dinner when he made the following statement: "What are the qualifications for public office? Well, first of all a man has to recognize he's a public serpent."

*　　*　　*

A Missouri candidate for office, speaking of his opponent said, "That low-down scoundrel deserves to be kicked to death by a jackass—and I'm just the one to do it."

*　　*　　*

At a California Republican fund-raising dinner the chairman said, "I am happy to introduce our Chief Executioner, Governor George Duekmejian."

The same toastmaster introduced Senator Pete Wilson with, "For the last fifteen years, the Senator has been a lifelong resident of our state."

*　　*　　*

A South Carolina lieutenant governor spoke at a political affair: "I am not going to talk to you tonight in generalities. I am going to speak to you at random."

*　　*　　*

Some years ago a dinner was attended by the governor of the Virgin Islands who was visiting Washington. A well-known member of the cabinet served as the toastmaster. After the usual complimentary remarks he said, "And now it is a great pleasure to present the Virgin of Governor's Island."

*   *   *

An Alabama farmer, trying to win the Democratic nomination for Congress from that state, stood before a group and warned against the imposition of heavier tariffs on imports.

"If you can't stop shearing the wool off the sheep that lays the golden egg," he declared, "you'll pump it dry."

*   *   *

One evening at a banquet, a midwestern mayor said, "And Congressman Krantz is a public servant who is equal to few and superior to none."

*   *   *

A county supervisor speaking at a Lincoln Day dinner: ". . . and it is fitting to pay tribute to Abraham Lincoln, who was born in a log cabin that he built with his own hands."

*   *   *

A Virginia assemblyman spoke at a rally: "There are three subjects which now agitate our great state. The first is pollution. The second is our airport problem, and the third is the state prison. I shall pass over the first two briefly, as my feelings are well known, and move to the state prison, where I shall dwell for some time."

During a hot debate in the Delaware Legislature the Republican leader exclaimed: "In the words of the great Daniel Webster, who wrote the dictionary, 'Give me Liberty or give me death!' "

A colleague tugged at his coat and whispered, "Daniel Webster didn't write the dictionary; it was Noah."

"Noah, nothing," replied the speaker. "Noah built the ark!"

* * *

"Senator, your speech was superfluous, simply superfluous," said a woman admirer.

"I'm glad you liked it," he answered, "I hope to have it published posthumously."

"Wonderful!" she replied. "I hope it will be soon."

* * *

At a women's club luncheon the chairwoman announced, "We have intended to increase the dues this year, but now we won't have to, for we have been able to arrange for several cheap speakers, starting with Representative Ledford!"

* * *

Did you hear about the mint-flavored shoes for government officials who keep putting their feet in their mouths?

The candidate for governor summed up his speech like this: ". . . and that's my platform, ladies and gentlemen. It won't cost anybody anything unless they are taxpayers."

* * *

A congressman sent a page boy with a verbal message back to his office. An hour later, he summoned the boy to his desk and said: "Why didn't you deliver that message as I gave it to you?"

"I did the best I could," said the boy.

"You did the best you could?" yelled the politician. "You fouled up the whole thing. If I knew I was sending a jackass, I would have gone myself."

* * *

The beautiful Sea Ranch exec secretary Rita Kent tells about the chairwoman of the county Republican club who began her remarks: "We did not have to pay anything to get the senator here tonight, and after he speaks I am sure we will all agree he was worth every penny of it."

* * *

Then there was the memorable *faux pas* by Gerald Ford, "Whenever I can I always watch the Detroit Tigers on radio."

* * *

Richard Daley, Chicago's unflappable mayor, was a master word mixer. At a dinner, Daley once said: "We must restore to Chicago all the good things it never had."

He once introduced Carl Sandburg as the poet "lariat" of Chicago.

On another occasion the mayor opened his speech with: "Ladies and gentlemen of the League of Women Voters."

*   *   *

A United States senator broke up a gathering of English teachers with: "What I am going to tell you is more truth than poultry. The United States has got to rise to greater and greater platitudes of achievement."

*   *   *

Most Democrats will never forget the 1980 National Convention when Jimmy Carter referred to Hubert Humphrey as Hubert Horatio Hornblower.

*   *   *

And finally, one of the most quoted blunders, made by United Nations Ambassador Warren Austin when he suggested that Jews and Arabs resolve their differences "in a true Christian spirit."

Donkeys

"I think I'll have a Democrat drink."
"How do you make a Democrat drink?"
"Elect a Republican!"

*　　*　　*

Two committee chairmen, each a member of the opposite party, were at the same charity dinner. By chance, they entered the men's washroom at the same time. The Democrat washed his hands before urinating. The Republican washed his hands after he went.

"A good Republican," declared the local party leader, "learns to wash his hands *after* he relieves himself!"

"A good Democrat," said the other man, "learns not to piss on his hands."

*　　*　　*

"Would you contribute ten dollars to help bury a Republican?"

"Here's thirty dollars; bury three of them!"

*　　*　　*

Members of the opposite party will always be fighting. It's part of politics. Once a Republican congressman walked up to a Democrat after hearing him speak and shouted, "You can go to hell!"

"Thanks!" replied the Democrat, "that's the first time I was ever invited to Republican headquarters."

*　　*　　*

A staunch Democrat was driving through Wyoming when his car broke down. He was stranded in what was obviously Republican country, for no one would stop for him because he had a bumper sticker that said: VOTE DEMOCRATIC.

Finally, he tore off the sticker. Within five minutes a gorgeous blonde in a convertible stopped and picked him up. As they drove along her skirt worked its way higher and higher up her leg. Finally, he said, "Stop the car and let me out. Here I am, a Republican only five minutes and already I feel like screwing somebody."

*　　*　　*

REPUBLICAN SENATOR

Someone who can talk for an hour without saying anything—

Serve six years without knowing anything—

And get reelected without doing anything.

*　　*　　*

A Republican senator running for reelection was giving a speech on a college campus. "Mr. Chairman," he complained, "I have been on my feet nearly ten minutes, but there is so much shouting and interrupting, I can hardly hear myself speak."

"It's okay," shouted a student from the rear, "you ain't missin' much!"

*　　*　　*

After reading his prepared statement at a Republican party press conference, the blustering senator threw the meeting open for questions.

"It is true," asked one sarcastic reporter, "that you were born in a log cabin?"

"You're thinking of Abraham Lincoln," replied the senator coolly. "*I* was born in a manger."

*　　*　　*

The following scene took place in the home of the state Democratic chairman:

"Harriet," announced the man to his wife, "I'm going to find out what our son wants to be when he grows up. Watch."

The man put a twenty dollar bill on the table that stood for the banking business. Next to it he laid a Bible, representing the ministry. And beside the Bible he placed a bottle of whiskey, for a life as a bum.

The parents hid behind the drapes. Their ten-year-old son entered the room, picked up the bill, held it to the light, and replaced it. He fingered the pages of the Bible. Then he uncorked the bottle of booze and smelled the contents.

Then the boy quickly stuffed the twenty dollar bill in his pocket, tucked the Bible under his arm, grabbed the bottle and strolled out of the room.

"Heaven help us!" exclaimed the father. "He's going to be a Republican."

Republican Candidate: What we need is a working majority and then . . .

Democratic Voter: Better reverse it, mister. What you need is a majority working!

* * *

"Have you heard my last speech?" asked the aging Republican senator of a young constituent.

"I certainly hope so!" he replied.

* * *

REPUBLICAN
A person who loves the government
for all it is worth.

* * *

In a crowded Cleveland bar a man who had taken one too many stood up and shouted, "I'd gladly work a hundred times more for the Republicans than for anyone else."

A Republican supporter heard him, jumped up, clapped him on the back and said, "Good for you! But what line of business are you in?"

"I'm an undertaker."

* * *

The Congressman needed a secretary. The interviewing psychologist invited him down to watch the examination of candidates for the job. The psychologist called in the first girl and asked, "What's two and two?"

Her answer was prompt, "Four."

The second girl thought for a moment, suspecting a catch, and said, "Twenty-two."

The last applicant answered, "Four, but it could be twenty-two."

After they had gone, the psychologist said to the congressman, "The tests were very revealing. The first girl had a conventional mind: to her two and two always is four. The second girl has imagination: she realized it might be twenty-two. The third girl is a combination of both: she is practical and has imagination. Clearly she will make the best secretary. Now, which would you like?"

The congressman replied, "The one with the big tits!"

*   *   *

Senator to Clerk: I want every married woman in the constituency to read my message about women's rights.

Clerk: No problem. We'll address the letters to their husbands and mark them "personal."

*   *   *

Hubert Humphrey once said that he learned the hard way not to cross barbs with the late President Harry Truman.

He recalled a time when he was campaigning for the Senate and Harry Truman came through Missouri on a visit.

"I asked him how come Minnesota seemed to have all the Swedes and Missouri seemed to have all the mules," Humphrey said.

Harry fixed me with a steely eye and snapped, "I guess it's because Missouri had first choice."

*   *   *

A Democrat out on his motor
Ran down a Republican voter.
  "Thank goodness," he cried,
  "He was on the wrong side,
So I don't blame myself one iota."

*   *   *

Charlie met his friend Frank who was sporting three hats, one on top of another.

"What's the idea?" asked Charlie.

"I've decided to become a Republican," answered Frank.

"What the devil are you wearing three hats for?"

"A Republican has one hat to cover his head, another to toss in the ring, and one to talk through!"

*   *   *

The reporter walked into the newspaper office. "All right," said the editor, "what did our eminent Democratic statesman have to say?"

"Nothing."

"Well, keep it down to a column."

*   *   *

Some elections back, the phone rang at Democratic headquarters in Washington.

"Excuse me," said the voice, "can you please give me the name of the Republican candidate for governor in Montana?"

"Why don't you call the Republican National Committee?" suggested the clerk. "Surely they'll be able to give you the information."

"This *is* the Republican National Committee!" replied the voice meekly.

*   *   *

Republican: I would like to suggest that we dispense with mudslinging in this campaign.

Democrat: An excellent suggestion. If you will refrain from telling lies about the Democratic party, I will give you my assurance that I will withhold the truth about the Republican party.

*   *   *

Sam Seidman, the retired Brooklyn cabbie, got big tips from fares with this knee-slapper:

A Republican senator and a priest arrived at the pearly gates at the same time. Saint Peter threw open the gates, and shouted, "He's here! He's here!" As he led the politician inside, trumpets began to sound, flutes began to play and a chorus of angels sang a celestial greeting.

In the excitement, the priest was knocked down and the pearly gates slammed in his face. He knocked again. Saint Peter opened the gates, and let the priest enter.

"Saint Peter," cried the priest, "I have served God all my life, and dedicated myself to the salvation of mankind, yet you completely ignore me and give a great welcome to a *politician*!"

"Oh, Father, I am sorry!" exclaimed Peter. "See we get a great many priests up here but this is the first Republican senator we've ever had!"

In Florida a senator pleaded with the governor to procure him the renomination. This would almost automatically insure the senator's being reelected.

"I can't do that," said the governor. "It's your own fault. Even I couldn't get you reelected. Not after that story about the hotel episode in Miami."

"That story is a damned lie!" cried the politician. "Why there isn't even any Hotel Episode in Miami."

*   *   *

Candidate: I was born a Republican. I was reared a Republican and I shall die a Republican.

Voice from Back: Have you no ambition at all?

*   *   *

A group of congressmen were conferring. Said one, "We've got a $120 million appropriation to spend. What are we going to do with it?"

"I've got an idea on how to spend it!" said a Democrat. "How about building a bridge over the Mississippi River. Lengthwise!"

*   *   *

Most Republicans start out to do well—
and they end up well-to-do.

*　　*　　*

The Republican candidate for congress
announced at a huge outdoor rally: "I hate
to say this, but my opponent has a bad
reputation. He not only steals money, but
he drinks heavily and chases after women."

"That's great," piped a voice from the
crowd, "we won't have to break him in."

*　　*　　*

A congressman's wife was suing him
for divorce. He stood up in court and said,
"Your Honor, she's asking you to break up
our home because I committed adultery.
That's ridiculous! You know we Republicans never commit ourselves to anything."

The judge dismissed the case.

*　　*　　*

The Dean of Women at a prominent
midwestern college was introducing a visiting Republican senator to the students. In
tones of admiration, she said, "I couldn't
begin to tell you all of the senator's ac-
complishments, but as an indication you'll
be interested to know that he has a nine inch
Who's Who."

*　　*　　*

REPUBLICAN COMMITTEE

A group of men who individually
can do nothing, but collectively
can meet and decide that nothing
can be done.

*   *   *

Some years back a reporter approached
the governor of a western state.

"I'm going to ask you a very candid
question, sir. Are you going to run for
President?"

"And I'm going to give you a very
candid answer," replied the governor.

"Yes?"

"No comment."

*   *   *

If Ronald Reagan and Secretary Schultz
jumped off the Washington Monument at
the same time, which would land first?

Who cares?

*   *   *

"I guess you heard about Henry Kis-
singer's accident?

"No, what happened?"

"He was out taking his usual morning
walk and a motorboat hit him."

*　　*　　*

A New England Republican congressman was interviewed on his eightieth birthday."

"You've been in Congress a long time, haven't you, sir?" asked the reporter.

"I surely have. Comin' up forty-five years."

"And you must have seen some mighty big changes, right, sir?"

"Yes," replied the old man. "And I've been against 'em all."

*　　*　　*

A famous eastern mayor got out of a taxi in front of the Beverly Wilshire Hotel. "I suppose," he said, looking through his wallet for a new five dollar bill, "like a lot of other folks nowadays, you would rather have clean money?"

"That's okay," said the taxi driver, "I don't care how you make your dough."

*　　*　　*

"There are some things in your speech that I didn't quite understand," said a voter.

"Probably," replied the Republican senator. "Those were the topics I referred to in a confident offhand way to avoid disclosing that I don't understand them either."

*　　*　　*

Arleen Morelli, Home Federal's premier branch manager, pleasures this pastiche of persiflage:

A Pennsylvania state trooper stopped a speeding legislator on his way to Washington. Before the policeman could take out his ticket book, the congressman said: "Look officer, I admit I was going a bit fast, but I'd like to point out to you that I am a congressman . . ."

"Sorry," said the trooper. "Ignorance is no excuse."

A congressman and a minister were passing the time of day.

"Do you think a Democrat has a chance to get into heaven?" asked the lawmaker.

"I think so," said the cleric, "just so long as he gives his name and doesn't say another word."

*   *   *

An elderly congressman well known for his dalliances with the ladies was sitting beside a very pretty blonde at a Washington party. During the dinner, he put his hand under the table and started to feel her ankle.

She gave him a sweet smile. Encouraged, he went a little further and reached the calf of her leg and again the lady smiled. The congressman, thrilled by this encouragement, went above the knees.

Suddenly, giving the congressman a sweet smile she leaned and whispered in his ear, "When you get far enough to discover that I'm a man, don't change the expression on your face. I'm Secret Agent Number 18!"

*   *   *

Did you hear about the conscientious Democratic congressman and his recurrent nightmare?

He dreams that all the money he is spending is his own!

*   *   *

Here are some quips from the lips of a few dandy Democrats:

The administration has come out with a new tractor for farmers. It has no seats or steering wheel—because the poor guys have lost their behinds and have nowhere to turn.

—Senator Dennis DeConcini (Arizona)

An optimist is someone who believes in Reagonomics. A pessimist is someone who understands Reagonomics.

—Rep. Paul Simon (Illinois)

President Reagan is right. The country is picking up steam. Labor is steamed, home buyers are steamed, older citizens are steamed.

—Rep. Les Aspin (Wisconsin)

The Administration is trying to make Social Security a no-frills program. The problem is that their idea of a frill is eating.

—Rep. Claude Pepper (Florida)

*   *   *

A senator from one of the oil-producing states wandered into a foreign-car showroom. "May I be of help, sir?" asked the impeccably attired, haughty salesman.

"Yep," said the casually dressed and obviously self-made man of means. "My girlfriend has a touch of the flu. Watcha got in the way of a get-well car?"

* * *

Youngster:	Father, what is a traitor in politics?
Veteran Politician:	A traitor is a man who leaves the Democratic party and goes over to the other one.
Youngster:	Then what is a man who leaves the Republican party and comes over to you?
Veteran Politician:	A convert, my son!

* * *

The opponents at a huge rally included an incumbent Republican congressman (backed by excessive oil company profits) and a young Democratic school teacher. The oft-elected congressman rattled on about his service to the poor, his service to the elderly and his service to his country. (Not a word about his oil company association.) Then the young Democrat spoke:

"When I was a boy, my pa had a registered bull, and he was rented out for 'service' here, or being sent for 'service' there. I was mighty curious about what this 'service' was, but pa kept saying I was too young.

"One day my folks were away and a neighbor phoned and said he'd like to have our bull for awhile. I figured this'd be my chance to find out what 'service' was, so I brought the bull over myself.

"When I asked the neighbor if I could watch, just like my pa, he told me I was too young, so I left.

"But I sneaked back to the high board corral where they'd taken the bull and I found a knothole.

"Folks, it was through that knothole in that high board fence that I saw what the oil companies have been doing to the people of the United States for the past forty years."

He won by a landslide.

Flimflam Funnies

The Republican candidate rushed home and excitedly told his wife, "Darling, I've been elected."

"Honestly?"

"Why bring that up?"

*   *   *

A panhandler stopped a congressman on the street and asked him for a dime.

"A dime won't buy anything these days," said the lawmaker. "Don't you want a quarter?"

"No," replied the panhandler, "with all the shady politicians around today, I'm afraid to carry too much cash."

*   *   *

"Robin Hood used to rob the rich to give to the poor. Where would he be if he were alive today?"

"Well, if he did it in reverse, he'd be in Washington."

*   *   *

FROM THE DIARY OF A GOVERNMENT OFFICIAL

First year: All men are good.
Second year: Some men are good.
Third year: A few men are crooks.
Fourth year: Most men are crooks.
Fifth year: All men are crooks—so I might as well take my share too.

*   *   *

Granby graduated from American University with a political science degree. His father, a respected circuit judge, provided him with his first political advice: "Son, remember, there's a difference between Democrats and Republicans. Democrats will steal a hot stove. Republicans put their gloves on first."

*   *   *

A young Nebraska lawyer won a seat in that state's House of Representatives. He immediately approached his father, the Democratic state chairman, and requested advice on what to do in time of trouble.

"Well, son," said the Democratic boss, "the first rule is: Don't get caught at whatever it is.

"The second rule is: If you get caught, don't admit a thing.

142

"If they press you," continued the boy's father, "point at something else. Plead innocence. That's the third rule.

"The fourth rule," proclaimed the veteran Democrat, "is one you use in sheer desperation: Deny everything, wrap yourself in the American flag, tell them you have a sick mother, get yourself a good lawyer, and start looking for another job."

* * *

"Dad, are political plums raised from seeds?"

"No, son. It's done by grafting."

* * *

A newspaper editor had to correct his youthful reporter.

"Never say that every member of the Third Ward Political Club takes graft."

"But they all do."

"Yes, I know," said the editor, "but let's avoid trouble. Say that every member of the club, with one exception, takes graft. Then no member of the club will feel personally offended."

* * *

SIXTH WARD SERENADE

I Get A Kick-Back Out of You

* * *

"I just found out why the Republicans win in our town all the time!"

"Why?"

"Yesterday, somebody broke into the mayor's office and found next year's election returns."

*   *   *

Everybody in town expressed surprise when a crooked lawyer was elected to the City Council. "I can't understand," said a voter, "how a crook like you could get elected."

"I'll admit," said the lawyer, "that everyone knows I'm on the shady side. But they also know my opponent is a crook, too. It just happens that he knows more people than I do, and they voted for me to keep him out of office."

*   *   *

Did you hear about the politician who was elected because of his gift of gab?

He was later defeated because of his gift of grab!

*   *   *

"Why is it," asked a reporter, "that politicians very seldom tell the truth?"

"Well," said the old politician, "there just ain't that much truth around."

*   *   *

Livermore lost his quest for a second term as mayor. A friend asked, "What happened?"

"Well, the people just wouldn't reelect me because of my youth."

"But you're over fifty-years-old and your youth has been spent," said the friend.

"That's the trouble," said the ex-mayor. "They found out how I spent it."

* * *

Republican: The mayor stole the last election.
Democrat: No, he didn't.
Republican: He did, too.
Democrat: No, he paid cash money for it.

* * *

Swenson, a Minnesota farmer, had just butchered a hog. After dressing it down he hung the two halves in his barn.

During the night somebody busted into the barn and stole half of the hog. The next day Swenson told a neighbor of his misfortune.

"Some damn Republican must've broke in and stole half my hog," he complained.

"How do you know it was a Republican?" asked the other Minnesotan.

"Simple," replied the farmer. "If it'd been a Democrat who broke in, he'd have stolen the whole hog."

* * *

Spinelli went to an old-time Cook County political rally, held in a smoke-filled Chicago hotel ballroom. Ten minutes after his arrival he discovered that his watch had disappeared. Spinelli went to the man in charge of the affair and told him that someone had stolen his watch.

"Who were you standing next to?" asked the man.

Spinelli looked out over the room and whispered: "Next to that fella in-a the blue and red shirt."

"Wait here," he said. "I'll be right back."

In a few minutes he returned and handed Spinelli his watch. "Thanks," said the Italian. "What did the pickpocket say?"

"Shh! He doesn't know I got it."

POLITICIAN'S POEM

All type of politicos you meet,
They work for state and county,
To get such jobs is quite a feat
There's no mutiny on the public bounty.

* * *

Democrat: Your man Lynch is so crooked that the wool he pulls over
your eyes is half cotton.

Republican: Your man Cosgrave is so crooked that if he swallowed a nail
it'd come out a corkscrew.

* * *

A candidate was running for county
commissioner in a rural Iowa community.
Two farmers were discussing him.

"Clete, you're a neighbor of this feller,
now is he honest?"

"Well," said the other farmer. "I
wouldn't exactly call him a liar. But I heard
when he wants his hogs to come for feed,
he has someone else call 'em."

* * *

Politician at Election Meeting: "I never
stole anything in my life. All I ask in this
election is a chance."

* * *

A candidate for Congress was campaigning in a Kansas farm district. He stopped at a barn where a young maid was milking a cow. In a few minutes, a voice came from the nearby house, "Who's there in the barn with you, Alma?"

"A man," replied the girl.

"What kind of man?"

"A politician, Mama."

"Alma, you come right in the house this minute!" shouted the woman. "And bring the cow in with you!"

* * *

Did you hear about the Maryland governor who never took a bribe—unless it was in cash?

* * *

Farmers are tough constituents for politicians, particularly those campaigning for office. Farmers know that when a bull is brought in to mate with a cow, it is called "servicing the cow."

"So," observed a New England farmer, "when you hear of some politician who says he wants to do public service, you know exactly what he means."

* * *

Louise Sill, the popular Hancock Park homemaker, applauds this harvest of high-jinks:

Tracy and Wood, two senior citizens, were strolling through the cemetery of a large New England city. Suddenly they stopped at a stone that read:

HERE LIES A POLITICIAN
AND AN HONEST MAN

"Can you imagine that," said Tracy, "two people in one grave!"

*   *   *

Years ago in West Virginia members of the legislature were known to grab anything that smelled of cash. As a gag, one of the honest members placed a notice on the washroom door.

FOUND

*A ten dollar bill in the
House Chamber.
Owner please claim.*

Next day, the honest legislator told friends, "I got twelve calls from colleagues who claimed they lost the money and demanded I return it."

*   *   *

SOUTHERN SMALL TOWN
NEWSPAPER STORY

The rumor that our councilman is an escaped convict has been officially denied by his party. He did, in fact, serve all his sentence, according to a government spokesman.

*   *   *

"Today we can rent anything. Rent a boat, rent a car, rent a home, rent a plane, rent a husband."

"Yeah, the only thing you can't rent is a politician. You still have to buy them."

*   *   *

A convict's wife visited him once a month in prison. During one visit, he asked anxiously, "What's the news on the governor's pardon?"

"It couldn't be better," she answered brightly. "He's getting out next Tuesday!"

*   *   *

Did you hear about the politician who was so crooked that he could hide in the shadow of a corkscrew, and when he died they had to screw him into the ground?

*   *   *

Greg Getschman, Chicago's masterful literary associate, likes this loony lulu:

President Johnson, Vice President Humphrey, and the Windy City's Mayor Daley were aboard a yacht that sank in a storm. They were the only survivors washed up on a desert island.

A decision had to be made on which way to walk in the hope of finding food and water.

"Let's go to the left," said President Johnson.

"No," said Vice President Humphrey. "I think we should go to the right."

"Gentlemen," said Mayor Daley, "I think we should go straight ahead."

"Well," said LBJ, "I am the President and I say go left."

"Just a minute," said Humphrey, "on this island I believe we each have an equal say, and I say go right."

"Wait," said Mayor Daley, "I suggest we hold a secret ballot." They did.

Mayor Daley won by a vote of eight to two.

SENATOR'S EXPENSE ACCOUNT

She was "honeychile" in New Orleans
The hottest of the bunch;
But on the old expense account,
She was gas, cigars and lunch.

* * *

Then there was the politician who managed his life on the cafeteria plan—self-service only!

* * *

"How did the audience receive your campaign speech when you told them you had never bought a vote?" the campaign chairman asked the Republican candidate for governor.

"A few cheered, but the majority seemed to lose interest," he replied.

Elephants

"My next-door neighbor is a staunch Republican."

"How can you tell?"

"Every Christmas on his front lawn he has a scene that shows Joseph leading Mary into Bethlehem on an elephant."

*   *   *

"Which way to the rest room?" asked the Republican senator.

"Just around the corner," replied the attendant.

"Don't hand me any of that Democratic propaganda—I'm in a hurry!"

*   *   *

A Democrat stands for what he thinks the public will fall for.

*   *   *

The main attraction of a small circus was a donkey that performed a number of feats and wound up its performance by bursting into tears. But at a matinee one afternoon the trainer couldn't get his donkey to do any weeping.

A man in the audience went down and offered to help the trainer. He whispered into the donkey's ear and soon the animal began weeping and wailing as never before.

"What did you say to that animal?" asked the trainer.

"Just the facts of life," said the stranger. "I told him the size of the national debt, the annual interest charge on it, the high taxes on individual incomes, the cost of armaments and foreign aid, the cost of congressional junkets, and some other things the Democrats are responsible for. It's enough to make even a jackass cry!"

*   *   *

"What would be a good way to raise revenue and still benefit the people?"

"Tax every political speech made by a Democrat in this country."

*   *   *

REPUBLICAN'S RECOLLECTION

My campaign was a pleasant one,
And worthy here of note;
I only kissed the babies who
Were old enough to vote.

*   *   *

Several top-ranking Democrats had a secret meeting at an exclusive Washington club to decide strategy for beating a bill they all detested. As they got down to business, they noticed that the waiter was stationed near the door. And he refused to leave.

"If you don't scram this minute," shouted one red-faced congressman, "I'm gonna report you to the manager of this club."

"It was the manager who ordered me to stay here," replied the waiter. "He's holding me responsible for the silverware."

*   *   *

A congressman from the deepest South was aiming both barrels at sex education in the schools recently. "I don't want my twelve-year-old son to hear such filth," he proclaimed. "I've made my stand on this issue since the day the stork brought the little fellow."

*   *   *

DEMOCRATIC TAXIDERMIST

He stuffs ballot boxes.

* * *

At a high level meeting, the head of the central Democratic committee was receiving reports from the chairmen of county committees.

"Things never looked better for a clean sweep for the Democratic ticket than they do this fall," reported one country leader. "It's dollars to doughnuts that we'll even elect the candidate for judge of probate."

"What makes that so important?" asked the top Democratic politico.

"Well, several years ago the Republicans put up a man who had only one arm and we've never been able to overcome the appeal of that empty sleeve. But he's out this time, boys! We Democrats have nominated a man who is paralyzed from his neck up!"

* * *

Democrats divide their time between passing laws and helping their friends evade them.

* * *

Norman Palm, the Wyoming sheep ranching biggie, wins warm smiles with this whimsical winner:

A Democrat candidate, in a house-to-house canvass, was trying to persuade a man to vote for the ticket.

"No," said the voter, "my father was a Republican and so was my grandfather, and I won't vote anything but the Republican ticket."

"That's no argument," said the candidate. "Suppose your father and your grandfather had been horse thieves—would that make you a horse thief?"

"No," came the answer. "I suppose in that case, I'd be a Democrat!"

*　　*　　*

The congressman summoned one of his secretaries.

When she sat comfortably in her chair he said, "You've been here two months now and I'm glad to note that your typing has improved miraculously. However, it's not so good that you can stop wearing those tight sweaters yet!"

*　　*　　*

"What makes you think the Democratic senator is conceited?

"Well, on his last birthday he sent his parents a telegram of congratulations."

*　　*　　*

Sam Tenney, the superb Sea Ranch golf supervisor, sends players out with this sidesplitter:

O'Connor knelt in the confessional, "Yes, my son?" said the priest as he slid open the partition.

"Bless me, Father, for I have sinned," O'Connor whispered. "Yesterday I killed two Democratic election workers . . ."

"I'm not interested in your politics," interrupted the priest. "Just tell me your sins!"

Two lions escaped from the zoo in Washington D.C. and didn't meet again for three months. One was sleek and fat and the other nothing but skin and bones.

"You certainly look well fed," said the emaciated one. "How did you ever manage?"

"Nothing to it," answered the fat one. "I've been holed up at the House Office Building, eating a Democratic congressman or two a day. So far nobody's noticed it."

*   *   *

A Democratic congressman, anxious for some much needed lovemaking, climbed into bed with his wife. Before the legislator could get started, she began complaining about economic conditions in the country.

"Everything is going up," she whined. "The price of food, the cost of clothes, the beauty shop. I'd be happy if just one thing would go down."

"You just got your wish," came the sleepy reply.

*   *   *

Two Pentagon stenos were chatting over coffee. "The new chief is fantastic. And he dresses so well."

"Yes. And so quickly too!"

*   *   *

DEMOCRATIC POLITICIAN

A guy who works up his gums at election time and gums up the works forever after.

* * *

Two men were sitting beside each other on a train.

"I just got out of prison this morning," one traveler told his seat companion. "It's going to be tough facing old friends."

"I understand what you mean," said the Democratic lawmaker beside him. "I'm just getting home from Congress."

* * *

Phillips and Funston were on the main street of a New England town discussing the coming election. "I don't want to vote for any of the candidates," said Phillips. "I don't know any of them."

"I don't know what to do either," answered Funston, "I know all of them."

* * *

The secretary of agriculture was a noted wit. Once a heckler shouted at him: "How many toes has a pig?"

The secretary quipped back: "Take off your shoes and count."

* * *

Greg Chapman, Beverly Hills's classy custom clothier, cracks up customers with this rib-tickler:

A GOP Senator was regaling a banquet audience one evening when a heckler disturbed the smooth flow of his oratory.

The legislator frowned, and then said, "When I was a lad back on the farm, my dad once gave me for my birthday a wonderful little donkey. 'See that he's properly fed, curried down and bedded. And always end up by locking the barn door,' he told me.

"Well, gentlemen, there came an evening, unfortunately, when I forgot to lock the barn door. The donkey walked out and got himself run over by a truck. My dad looked sadly at the carcass and said, 'Son, that animal's going to haunt you for the rest of your life.' And my dad sure hit the nail on the head."

The senator pointed to the heckler and said, "There sits that jackass now!"

Pickett, a young Democrat just entering politics, accepted an invitation to speak at a hard-nosed conservative club dinner.

The liberal aspirant promised the usual cradle-to-grave legislation if he were elected.

When Pickett got home, his wife asked how he had made out with his speech. "I knocked 'em in the aisles," he said. "Honey, when I finished my talk, they said they were going to invite me back to speak again next winter."

"Really?" asked the wife.

"Yes," said the young Democrat, "when I stepped down from the stage, the chairman came up to me and said: 'Pickett, it'll be a damn cold night when we invite you back again.' "

*   *   *

A state employee in California was driving a state truck along the freeway when he was flagged down by a trooper. "Don't you know you were going seventy miles an hour?"

"No, I didn't," said the driver.

"Haven't you a governor on that truck?"

"No, sir," said the employee. "The governor's in Sacramento; that's fertilizer you smell."

*   *   *

Abe Lincoln wouldn't have any trouble getting an education today.

He'd have been a cinch for a scholarship as a basketball center.

*   *   *

AT A DEMOCRATIC STREET RALLY

Candidate: We must get rid of radicalism, socialism, bolshevism, communism and anarchism.

Voice From Crowd: And while we're about it, why not throw out rheumatism?

*   *   *

Robert Dole, the senator from Kansas, pleases listeners with his self-effacing humor. When people asked him how he took the defeat for presidential nominee he replied, "I slept like a baby; I cried every hour on the hour."

Senator Dole loves telling how a radio announcer once summed up his background: "Senator Dole was born and raised in Kansas, served in World War II, suffered a serious head injury, after which he went into politics."

*   *   *

Not all joke tellers earn their living in show biz. Funny politicians are becoming the norm rather than the exception. Legislators have learned that you can get better results by getting a laugh. Here are a handful by the party's best known Republicans:

Senator Alan Simpson (R-Wyoming) often opens his talks with: "I know you want to hear the latest dope from Washington, D.C.—and here I am."

Senator Robert Kasten (R-Wisconsin) says a man called his office and asked how long it was going to take to stop inflation. "My secretary said, 'Just a moment, sir.' And the man said, 'That'll be fine,' and hung up."

*   *   *

Representative John LeBoutiller (R-New York) comments: "I'm a loyal Republican. I support the President when he's right—and I just keep quiet the other ninety-five percent of the time."

Charles Percy, GOP senator from Illinois, explained why his wife had written K.I.S.S. on a note card before he went on the *Today Show:* "It meant 'Keep it short, stupid.' "

*   *   *

John H. Chaffee, the Republican senator from Rhode Island, receives roars when relating this roaster:

"Rhode Island is a Democratic state. There's no getting around that. During one of my gubernatorial reelection campaigns, I was asked to give a Lincoln Day speech in one of the more rural sections of the state. After giving what I thought to be a real stem-winder to a packed hall of twelve Republicans, I was approached by a man in disheveled clothing.

"That was a lousy speech," he said. Just then, the town's GOP chairman quickly hustled the man away, saying to me, "Don't mind him, governor. He's just the town fool—he just repeats everything he hears."

*   *   *

Did you hear about the aspiring party member who fell in love with a girl at second sight?

The first time he saw her he didn't know she was the daughter of a senator.

*   *   *

To a young Republican, Dwight Eisenhower offered this advice:

"Never make people laugh. If you would succeed in life you must be as solemn as an ass. All the great monuments are built over solemn asses!"

*   *   *

An exquisite looking brunette floated into the office of a well-known Republican senator one morning and told his secretary that she came on personal business. When the young beauty was admitted to see the legislator, she blushed and said, "When my grandmother visited Washington, many years ago, Daniel Webster was here and he kissed her. Grandma loved telling us kids about it. Now that I'm visiting Washington—would you kiss me so I could have something to tell my own grandchildren?"

The senator leaped to fill the brunette's request and in a moment both had their clothes off. As they were making love, the door opened, a flashbulb went off and a man with a camera said: "Nice pose, Senator. That'll cost you five thousand bucks."

The senator, realizing his hopeless position, forked over the cash. As the brunette headed for the door, she said, "I—I'm sorry it turned out this way."

"It's all right," said the senator. "But tell me, how much did it cost Daniel Webster?"

A thunderstorm was raging over Washington D.C. Little Bobby woke up in terror and ran into his parent's bedroom.

"Daddy!" he cried, shaking his congressman father awake. "Why is it thundering?"

"Well," said his father, "every time someone tells a really big lie, heaven gets angry and it thunders."

"But isn't everyone asleep at this time of night?"

"Yes, but it's about this time that they print the *Washington Post*."

*   *   *

DYNAMIC DEMOCRAT

A fellow who finds out how the people are going, then takes a short cut across a field, gets out in front and makes them think he is leading the way.

*   *   *

Here's a letter the syndicated advice columnist never printed:

Dear Abby:

I've been a marine in Lebanon. My mother has epilepsy, and my father's laid up with heart trouble, so they can't work. My two sisters are the sole support of the family. They are hookers in Las Vegas. My only brother is in the pen for murder and rape. I have two cousins who are Democrats. I'm from the South and now that I'm out of uniform I naturally want to go back home to live.

My problem is this: I am in love with a belly dancer in a town near ours and I want to ask her to be my wife. Should I tell her about my two no-good Democrat cousins?

CONFUSED

*   *   *

Arizona Senator Barry Goldwater ribs his conservative image: "I was once offered a movie contract with Eighteenth Century Fox.

"I only fly on planes with two right wings."

Long after his thorough trouncing by Lyndon Johnson for the presidency, Goldwater said, "I have been called an extremist. That's not quite true. I go to extremes only when I'm arranging for my own defeat."

*   *   *

A Republican member of the House of Representatives and his wife were fast asleep in their upstairs bedroom. Suddenly, she began shaking him. "Wake up!" she shouted. "I think there's a robber in the house!"

"Impossible!" said her half-asleep husband. "In the Senate maybe, but never in the House."

*   *   *

Marci Manderscheid, San Francisco State's dynamic extension program director, doubles up over this doozy:

Two elderly Democratic senators got into a heated argument over a new piece of legislation. Finally, one of them shouted: "You talk about the Constitution. Why, I'll bet you a hundred dollars you can't recite the first words of the preamble to the Constitution."

"You got a bet!" replied the other. And he started, "I pledge allegiance . . ."

"Here's your hundred," interrupted the other. "I didn't think you'd know it."

Political Prattle

Lawyers are kidded about their ethics. Doctors are poked fun at for the way they practice medicine. Ethnic groups are ridiculed for stereotypical characteristics. Celebrities from the world of sports and show business are constantly being joked about. So it is only fair that politicians come in for their share of lampooning. Here are some timeless one-liners:

America is the only country where you can go on TV and kid politicians, and where politicians go on TV and kid the people.

*　　*　　*

The reason politicians make such strange bedfellows is because they all like the same bunk.

*   *   *

The mistake a lot of politicians make is to forget they've been appointed and think they've been anointed.

*   *   *

The average politician is a Liberal and Conservative. Liberal with your money, conservative with his.

*   *   *

A politician is a man who approaches every subject with an open mouth.

*   *   *

The gifted politician is the one who can give the type of answer that makes you completely forget the question.

*   *   *

Most politicians say what they think without thinking.

*   *   *

A politician who tries to please everybody often looks like a small puppy dog trying to follow four boys at the same time.

*　　*　　*

Success formula for politicians—long hours, short memories.

*　　*　　*

The problem with today's politicians who claim they'll build you a pie in the sky is that they're using your dough.

*　　*　　*

Why do politicians invent lies about each other when the truth would be bad enough?

*　　*　　*

There are two sides to every question and a good politician takes both.

*　　*　　*

It isn't necessary to fool all of the people all of the time—only during election campaigns.

*　　*　　*

A politician nominated at a state convention said that he was so surprised by the nomination that his acceptance speech fell out of his pocket!

A public official can fool some of the people all of the time, and all of the people some of the time, but not his private secretary.

*   *   *

A politician doesn't have to fool all of the people all of the time—he only has to fool a majority.

*   *   *

A skilled politician is one who can stand up and rock the boat and then make you believe he is the only one who can save you from the storm.

*   *   *

WASHINGTON D.C.

A city where many a politician is waiting to be discovered, and many are afraid they might be.

*   *   *

Some politicians are like the bottom half of a double boiler—they let off a lot of steam when they don't even know what's cooking.

*   *   *

ADVICE TO A POLITICIAN: Always be sincere whether you mean it or not.

*   *   *

The polls are places where you stand in line for a chance to decide who will spend your money.

*   *   *

To err is human. To blame it on someone else is politics.

Other Books by Larry Wilde

in paperback

THE OFFICIAL BEDROOM/BATHROOM
   JOKE BOOK
MORE THE OFFICIAL DEMOCRAT/
   REPUBLICAN JOKE BOOK
MORE THE OFFICIAL SMART KIDS/
   DUMB PARENTS JOKE BOOK
THE OFFICIAL BOOK OF SICK JOKES
MORE THE OFFICIAL JEWISH/IRISH
   JOKE BOOK
THE *LAST* OFFICIAL ITALIAN
   JOKE BOOK
THE OFFICIAL CAT LOVERS/
   DOG LOVERS JOKE BOOK
THE OFFICIAL DIRTY JOKE BOOK
THE *LAST* OFFICIAL POLISH
   JOKE BOOK
THE OFFICIAL GOLFERS JOKE BOOK
THE OFFICIAL SMART KIDS/DUMB
   PARENTS JOKE BOOK
THE OFFICIAL RELIGIOUS/NOT SO
   RELIGIOUS JOKE BOOK
THE OFFICIAL DEMOCRAT/
   REPUBLICAN JOKE BOOK
MORE THE OFFICIAL POLISH/ITALIAN
   JOKE BOOK
THE OFFICIAL BLACK FOLKS/WHITE
   FOLKS JOKE BOOK

THE OFFICIAL VIRGINS/SEX MANIACS
  JOKE BOOK
THE OFFICIAL JEWISH/IRISH
  JOKE BOOK
THE OFFICIAL POLISH/ITALIAN
  JOKE BOOK

and in hardcover

THE COMPLETE BOOK OF
  ETHNIC HUMOR
HOW THE GREAT COMEDY WRITERS
  CREATE LAUGHTER
THE GREAT COMEDIANS TALK
  ABOUT COMEDY

I love humor. I've spent over thirty years studying, analyzing, researching, teaching, performing and writing it. The fascination started in Jersey City where I was born in 1928. As a kid during the Depression we had to scratch real hard to make a buck and making jokes was a way of life. Particularly, the humor of politics for I grew up throughout the reign of Democratic boss Mayor Frank Hague.

After a two year stint in the Marine Corps where I found I could make leathernecks laugh, I worked my way through the University of Miami, Florida, doing a comedy act at the hotels. After graduating I entertained in night clubs and hotels all over the U.S. I got to play Vegas and Tahoe and the other big time spots being the ''supporting'' comedian for Ann-Margret, Debbie Reynolds, Pat Boone and a lot of others.

I've done acting roles on *Mary Tyler Moore*, *Rhoda*, *Sanford & Son* and other sitcoms; performed on Carson, Griffin, Douglas and did a bunch of TV commercials.

This is my thirtieth joke book. I'm also proud of the two serious works I've done on comedy technique: *The Great Comedians Talk About Comedy* and *How The Great Comedy Writers Create Laughter*. Both books have been called ''definitive'' works on the subject.

My books have sold over seven million copies which makes them the largest selling humor series in publishing history. And while I'm blowing my own horn here, the best thing I ever did was to marry Maryruth Poulos, a really talented writer from Wyoming.

Larry Wilde